THE STRANGE GENTLEMAN
AND OTHER PLAYS

by

CHARLES DICKENS

With an Introduction by

JEFFERY TILLETT

HEINEMANN EDUCATIONAL
BOOKS LTD · LONDON

Heinemann Educational Books Ltd

LONDON EDINBURGH MELBOURNE AUCKLAND TORONTO
HONG KONG   KUALA LUMPUR   SINGAPORE
JOHANNESBURG   NAIROBI   IBADAN
NEW DELHI

ISBN 0 435 23225 8

Published by
Heinemann Educational Books Ltd
48 Charles Street, London W1X 8AH

Printed in Great Britain by
Morrison & Gibb Ltd, London and Edinburgh

CONTENTS

FOREWORD

The Dickens' Centenary Celebrations of 1970 included several performances at repertory theatres in different parts of the country of his short farces. It must have come as a surprise to many of his readers to know—or to be reminded—that Dickens not only spent a considerable time on dramatics—amateur, though of a high order—but also wrote and collaborated in the writing of plays.

In point of fact Dickens wrote three one-act plays in full, provided the libretto for a comic opera, and collaborated in four other pieces, three of these being full length plays, chiefly the work of his friend and fellow novelist, Wilkie Collins.

This present collection reproduces four of his shorter farces: the first, from which this volume takes its title, in two acts, the other three each in one act. It is the hope of the editor that their publication will encourage performances by 'accomplished amateurs'—in exactly the same way that Dickens himself presented them, and of which he would most certainly have approved.

They present little difficulty in performance: they were not written with particularly subtle effects in mind, nor did they require very complicated settings. The latter could be either on flats and backcloths (as they were in Dickens' day) or in the more realistic style of the later nineteenth century. Like most playwrights of the period Dickens introduced songs into his plays: these can either be omitted where they occur or other suitable items substituted; perhaps from Victorian opera, especially from the works of Gilbert and Sullivan.

May I in conclusion thank the Librarians of the County Borough of Derby and the University of Nottingham for assistance I have received from them, and Mr. Edward Thompson for his encouragement throughout.

CHARLES DICKENS
AND THE THEATRE

Charles Dickens' interest in the theatre was awoken early
in his childhood. One of his most treasured toys was a
model theatre which he loved to operate—complete with
sound effects. His parents, though never well off, certainly
took him to pantomimes each Christmas. As a young boy,
he tells us, he saw the great Grimaldi himself. At about
the age of ten he was befriended by an older cousin, a
keen playgoer, James Lamert (the same young man who
later obtained for him a temporary job in the family
business sticking labels on pots of blacking when the
Dickens family fell onto hard times). James Lamert was
enthusiastic about the theatre and took his young cousin
to plays at the Theatre Royal, Chatham. Here Charles
first saw Shakespeare's plays, albeit rather inept productions of the sort he was later to poke fun at in such novels
as *Nicholas Nickleby* and *Great Expectations*. It was about
this time too that he first took up acting. In his *Life of
Charles Dickens*, John Forster, his friend and biographer,
tells us that as a schoolboy young Charles produced and
took part in a version of *The Miller and His Men*, a highly
popular and spectacular melodrama of the period, before
a family audience. A few years later he wrote and acted
in a parody of Shakespeare's *Othello*, again for a private
performance given by and for his family and his circle of
friends. Unfortunately no copy of this manuscript exists.

Later when he started work, first as a clerk in an
attorney's office, and later as a reporter, he found the
opportunity to extend his experience of the stage and
together with his friends would often attend the smaller
private theatres which then abounded in London.

At that time only three London theatres—those in

Covent Garden, the Haymarket and the Drury Lane—were licensed to present straight plays. Enterprising producers and managers, therefore, outsmarted the Law by presenting 'burlettas'—that is, plays with songs interspersed, rather like comic operas. The young Dickens must have seen many such productions—perhaps he even took part in them occasionally. His early essays often recall these experiences, for they provided material for Dickens' sense of humour and flair for mimicry in the way that he would burlesque the often pitiful performances, directing the barbs of his wit at both actor and audience.

As a young actor Charles Dickens was highly thought of and was reputed to have had a good singing voice as well as a natural gift for acting, particularly in melodramatic heavy parts, or in one-act farces. In fact, in 1832, then aged twenty, he sought and was even granted an audition at Covent Garden for a small part in a play called *The Hunchback*. Fate intervened, however, and a heavy cold prevented him from attending the audition; so Charles Dickens the famous novelist was not lost to posterity for Mr. C. Dickens the long-forgotten actor.

Though never well off the Dickens family were generous, kind and sociable, and entertained a cultured circle of friends. Charles' sister Fanny was at this time—the early 1830s—a singing student at the Royal Academy of Music, and introduced to the family circle many talented young artists and musicians. Among these was the composer John Hullah, then a teacher at the Academy.

Dickens' friendship with John Hullah bore immediate fruit for during the Summer and Autumn of 1836 the two collaborated on a two-act comic-opera *The Village Coquettes*, Dickens writing the libretto and Hullah composing the music. Sheridan in the previous century had written a play with songs (*The Duenna*) and thus Dickens' burletta was a direct link between the work of Sheridan and the comic operas of Gilbert and Sullivan written in the latter half of the nineteenth century. It is interesting to conjecture what might have been produced if Dickens and Hullah had pursued their 'words and Music' relationship. But this did not happen for this was to be the first and last libretto that Dickens ever wrote, although *The Village Coquettes* was an immense success when it was staged in December 1836, and it was often revived subsequently.

An evening at the Victorian theatre was a long and entertaining affair. As well as the main play there were always two or three shorter pieces presented before and after it. Dickens wrote such a play as a companion piece to *The Village Coquettes*. It was called *The Strange Gentleman* and was based on one of his short stories, *The Great Winglebury Duel*, which had appeared in his *Sketches by Boz*. It had, in fact, already been produced successfully in the previous September, also as an item added to a bill.

Adaptations for the stage of novels and short stories were a common feature of the Theatre at that time. Programmes were changed frequently, usually weekly, and speed was essential for the playwright hacks who were employed for a weekly wage to turn out pieces for a resident repertory company. Dickens ingeniously showed that adaptation need not always be a one-way traffic for, in 1838, he wrote an original one-act play *The Lamplighter* which was never performed publicly and which, three years later, he, therefore, turned into a short story as *The Lamplighter's Tale*.

Dickens' early plays, all farces, were performed at the St. James's Theatre where John Braham, the singer, and a personal friend of Dickens, was manager in the 1830s. Braham no doubt detected Dickens' melodramatic strain and theatrical talent early in his career, and he gave the young man every encouragement. At this time Dickens was already famous as the author of *The Pickwick Papers*, and *Oliver Twist* was in the process of being serialized. A successful novelist had a more secure profession than a writer of one-act farces, soon to be forgotten—this certainly explains why Dickens never considered writing plays for a living, but only as something to be indulged in from time to time for the sheer fun of it, and for special occasions.

In 1844 Dickens took his family abroad to Italy, and settled in Genoa for a time. On his return to England in the following year he threw himself with tremendous energy into dramatic activities, and, together with his friend and biographer John Forster, acted in Ben Jonson's *Every Man in His Humour*. Dickens took the part of Captain Bobadil, as well as being stage manager. Two performances were given at a private London theatre in Dean Street, Soho, in aid of charity; later it was staged in a larger theatre. Dickens' amateur theatricals were glittering social occasions; evening dress was worn, and large sums were raised for various good causes.

In the years 1846–1850 Dickens spent less time on writing than at any other period of his life. True, he finished *Dombey and Son*, wrote several Christmas stories, and started *David Copperfield*. But his energies were principally given to the stage.

In 1848, he took on tour a production of *The Merry Wives of Windsor* in aid of funds for the Shakespeare Birthplace Trust. A series of one-act farces made up the bill, including Dickens' own *Is She His Wife?* which he had written over ten years earlier, in 1837. From London Dickens took his company to Birmingham and Manchester and then to Scotland. Stage management and travelling arrangements for the tour must have taken up a great deal of his time and energy at this period, quite apart from acting and producing, for he himself played the part of Justice Shallow in the Shakespeare play.

In 1851, the year of the Great Exhibition, Dickens reached the heights of his career as actor and stage manager for, on 27 May, Her Majesty Queen Victoria with Albert, the Prince Consort, honoured with her presence a performance given by Dickens' company at the Duke of Devonshire's London home. The play was Bulwer Lytton's *Not as Bad as We Seem* which the author, a great personal friend of Dickens, had written specially for the company. Several performances had been given already in aid of charitable causes, particularly those associated with letters and the theatre—such as those for writers and actors who had fallen on hard times, or who had died leaving widows and orphans without adequate provision. Compassion for those in straitened circumstances pervaded the pages of Dickens' novels: here he was showing that he could do something in a practical way to help them. He acted—literally!

In *Not as Bad as We Seem*, Dickens played the part of Lord Wilmot, an eighteenth-century fop. It was a part that gave full scope to Dickens' talent for mimicry, and his acting was highly praised, not least by members of the theatrical profession, particularly by William Macready, the great actor-manager of the time who was an intimate friend of Dickens. There is no doubt that Dickens was highly impressed by the way in which Macready was improving standards in the theatre where melodrama was, at that time, all the rage and a melodramatic style of acting—as Dickens' style certainly was!—the accepted manner on the stage.

For this same Royal Performance, Dickens wrote a one-act farce as a 'curtain-raiser'. This was *Mr. Nightingale's Diary*. His friend Mark Lemon co-operated with him in the writing of the play, and these two, together with the novelist Wilkie Collins, who later wrote two melodramas, *The Lighthouse* (1855) and *The Frozen Deep* (1857) specially for the Dickens' company, took leading parts in it too. Dickens played the part of Gabblewig, a role that demanded five different stage disguises, female as well as male, and it is said that he brought the house down with his impersonations.

Following the immense success—social and theatrical—of the Royal Performance, Dickens purchased Tavistock House (now demolished) in Tavistock Square, Bloomsbury. Here he was able to construct and operate his own private theatre, and amateur theatricals continued to occupy his leisure time there from 1851 until he sold it in 1860. It was in this period that he grew his famous beard to fit him for the role of a shipwrecked sailor in the Wilkie Collins' play *The Frozen Deep*, which received many successful performances in London—including another Royal Performance—and also went on tour in the provinces. It was while on such a tour, in Manchester, that Charles Dickens first met Ellen Ternan, the young actress whose friendship was to make such a difference to his domestic and social life. But that is another story.

A photograph taken in 1854 shows the Dickens troupe as it then was: six ladies and eighteen gentlemen. For his tours Dickens would sign on professional actors and actresses; the London performances were given by gifted amateurs like himself.

This frenzy of theatrical activity in the 1850s affected Dickens' novel writing. *Bleak House* which belongs to the early 1850s is easily the most melodramatic of his works; he found work on *Hard Times*, albeit his shortest novel, heavy going and something of a chore. During the later 1850s too he started to give public readings of his works, in which he was able to give full vent to his theatrical abilities and sense of showmanship. There can be no doubt that the overwork and sapping of his nervous energies at this period of his life contributed considerably to his sudden death in 1870.

The last play in which Dickens had any hand was a full-length play in five acts entitled *No Thoroughfare*, performed in the West End in December 1867, three years before Dickens' death. It was based upon a story of the same title written by Dickens for the Christmas edition of a magazine appearing at the same time. The play was almost entirely the work of Wilkie Collins, although Dickens' hand is clearly to be seen in a (very melodramatic) Prologue. Incidentally, this was the only dramatization of one of his own stories in which Dickens had any part, though there were plenty of inferior hacks at hand ready to seize upon his novels as soon as they were written (and sometimes even before he had completed their serialization) to turn them into plays. There were no copyright laws then to protect authors from such plagiarization.

Of course, plays based upon Dickens' novels have always been popular right up to the present time. Today, both on the cinema screen and on television, films of his books are often shown. Some have even been transmogrified into musical comedies! None of this is to be wondered at. The pages of Dickens' novels contain the very stuff of drama: plots with exciting twists, wonderful dialogue, brilliant characterization, a sense of 'theatre', mystery and melodrama, and, above all, a wide range of humour, from high comedy to low farce. There can be no doubt that, as a novelist, Charles Dickens must have visualized many of his scenes in terms of the stage. As a dramatist he knew only too well the conditions under which playwrights laboured for mercenary managements as this revealing extract from *Nicholas Nickleby* so very clearly shows:

'We'll have a new show-piece out directly,' said the manager. 'Let me see—peculiar resources of this establishment—new and splendid scenery—you must manage to introduce a real pump and two washing-tubs.'

'Into the piece?' said Nicholas.

'Yes,' replied the manager. 'I bought 'em cheap at a sale the other day, and they'll come in admirably. That's the London play. They look up some dresses, and properties, and have a piece written to fit 'em. Most of the theatres keep an author on purpose.'

'Indeed!' cried Nicholas.

'Oh yes,' said the manager, 'a common thing. It'll look very well in the bills in separate lines—Real pump!—Splendid tubs!—Great attraction!'

'What should I get for all this?' inquired Nicholas, after a few moments' reflection. 'Could I live by it?'

'Live by it!' said the manager, 'Like a prince! With your own salary, and your friend's, and your writings, you'd make—ah! you'd make a pound a week!'

'You don't say so!'

'I do indeed, and if we had a run of good houses, nearly double the money.'

Nicholas shrugged his shoulders; but sheer destitution was before him.

Without more deliberation, he hastily declared that it was a bargain, and gave Mr. Vincent Crummles his hand upon it.

JEFFERY TILLETT

Bramcote Hills
Nottingham

To Jon Whatson
and the members of
Nottingham Playhouse
Schools Touring Company

'Does no other profession occur to you, which a young man of your figure and address could take up easily, and see the world to advantage in?' asked the manager.

'No,' said Nicholas, shaking his head.

'Why, then, I'll tell you one,' said Mr. Crummles, throwing his pipe into the fire, and raising his voice. 'The stage.'

'The stage!' cried Nicholas, in a voice almost as loud.

'The theatrical profession,' said Mr. Vincent Crummles. 'I am in the theatrical profession myself, my wife is in the theatrical profession, my children are in the theatrical profession. I had a dog that lived and died in it from a puppy; and my chaise-pony goes on, in Timour the Tartar. I'll bring you out, and your friend too. Say the word. I want a novelty.'

'I don't know anything about it,' rejoined Nicholas, whose breath had been almost taken away by this sudden proposal. 'I never acted a part in my life, except at school.'

THE STRANGE GENTLEMAN

A Comic Burletta

IN TWO ACTS
[1836]

'There's genteel comedy in your walk and manner, juvenile
tragedy in your eye, and touch-and-go farce in your laugh,'
said Mr. Vincent Crummles. 'You'll do as well as if you had
thought of nothing else but the lamps, from your birth
downwards. You can be useful to us in a hundred ways. Think
what capital bills a man of your education could write for the
shop-windows.'

'Well, I think I could manage that department,' said
Nicholas.

'To be sure you could,' replied Mr. Crummles. ' "For
further particulars see small hand-bills"—we might have half
a volume in every one of 'em. Pieces too; why, you could
write us a piece to bring out the whole strength of the
company, whenever we wanted one.'

'I am not quite so confident about that,' replied Nicholas.
'But I dare say I could scribble something now and then, that
would suit you.'

CAST OF THE CHARACTERS

At St. James's Theatre, September 29, 1836

MR. OWEN OVERTON (*Mayor of a small town on the road to Gretna, and useful at the St. James's Arms*) . . . . Mr. Hollingsworth.

JOHN JOHNSON (*detained at the St. James's Arms*) . Mr. Sidney.

THE STRANGE GENTLEMAN (*just arrived at the St. James's Arms*) . . . . Mr. Harley.

CHARLES TOMKINS (*incognito at the St. James's Arms*) . . . . Mr. Forester.

TOM SPARKS (*a one-eyed 'Boots' at the St. James's Arms*) . . . . Mr. Gardner.

JOHN ⎫
TOM ⎬ *Waiters at the St. James's Arms* ⎧ Mr. Williamson.
WILL ⎭ ⎨ Mr. May.
⎩ Mr. Coulson.

JULIA DOBBS (*looking for a husband at the St. James's Arms*) . . . . Madame Sala.

FANNY WILSON (*with an appointment at the St. James's Arms*) . . . . Miss Smith.

MARY WILSON (*her sister, awkwardly situated at the St. James's Arms*) . . . Miss Julia Smith.

MRS. NOAKES (*the Landlady at the St. James's Arms*) . . . . Mrs. W. Penson.

CHAMBERMAID (*at the St. James's Arms*) . . Miss Stuart.

Miss Smith and Miss Julia Smith will sing the duet of
'I know a Bank', in 'The Strange Gentleman'.

COSTUME

MR. OWEN OVERTON.—*Black smalls, and high black boots. A blue body coat, rather long in the waist, with yellow buttons, buttoned close up to the chin, white stock; ditto gloves. A broad-brimmed low-crowned white hat.*

STRANGE GENTLEMAN.—*A light blue plaid French-cut trousers and vest. A brown cloth frock coat, with full skirts, scarcely covering the hips. A light handkerchief, and eccentric low-crowned broad-brimmed white hat. Boots.*

JOHN JOHNSON.—*White fashionable trousers, boots, light vest, frock coat, black hat, gloves, etc.*

CHARLES TOMKINS.—*Shepherd's plaid French-cut trousers; boots, mohair fashionable frock coat, buttoned up; black hat, gloves, etc.*

5

TOM SPARKS.—*Leather smalls, striped stockings, and lace-up half boots, red vest, and a Holland stable jacket; coloured kerchief, and red wig.*

THE WAITERS.—*All in black trousers, black stockings and shoes, white vests, striped jackets, and white kerchiefs.*

MARY WILSON.—*Fashionable walking dress, white silk stockings; shoes and gloves.*

FANNY WILSON.—*Precisely the same as Mary.*

JULIA DOBBS.—*A handsome white travelling dress, cashmere shawl, white silk stockings; shoes and gloves. A bonnet to correspond.*

MRS. NOAKES.—*A chintz gown, rather of a dark pattern, French apron, and handsome cap.*

SCENE.—A SMALL TOWN, ON THE ROAD TO GRETNA.

TIME.—PART OF A DAY AND NIGHT.

Time in acting.—One hour and twenty minutes.

THE STRANGE GENTLEMAN

ACT I

SCENE I.—*A Room at the St. James's Arms; Door in Centre, with a Bolt on it. A Table with Cover, and two Chairs*, R. H.

Enter MRS. NOAKES, C. DOOR.

MRS. NOAKES. Bless us, what a coachful! Four inside—twelve out; and the guard blowing the key-bugle in the fore-boot, for fear the informers should see that they have got one over the number. Post-chaise and a gig besides.—We shall be filled to the very attics. Now, look alive, there—bustle about.

Enter FIRST WAITER, *running*, C. DOOR.

Now, John.

FIRST WAITER (*coming down* L. H.). Single lady, inside the stage, wants a private room, ma'am.

MRS. NOAKES (R. H.). Much luggage?

FIRST WAITER. Four trunks, two bonnet-boxes, six brown-paper parcels, and a basket.

MRS. NOAKES. Give her a private room, directly. No. 1, on the first floor.

FIRST WAITER. Yes, ma'am. [*Exit* FIRST WAITER, *running*, C. DOOR.

Enter SECOND WAITER, *running*, C. DOOR.

Now, Tom.

SECOND WAITER (*coming down* R. H.). Two young ladies and one gentleman, in a post-chaise, want a private sitting-room d'rectly, ma'am.

MRS. NOAKES. Brother and sisters, Tom?

SECOND WAITER. Ladies are something alike, ma'am. Gentleman like neither of 'em.

MRS. NOAKES. Husband and wife and wife's sister, perhaps. Eh, Tom?

7

SECOND WAITER. Can't be husband and wife, ma'am, because I saw the gentleman kiss one of the ladies.

MRS. NOAKES. Kissing one of the ladies! Put them in the small sitting-room behind the bar, Tom, that I may have an eye on them through the little window, and see that nothing improper goes forward.

SECOND WAITER. Yes, ma'am. (*Going.*)

MRS. NOAKES. And Tom! (*Crossing to* L. H.)

SECOND WAITER (*coming down* R. H.). Yes, ma'am.

MRS. NOAKES. Tell Cook to put together all the bones and pieces that were left on the plates at the great dinner yesterday, and make some nice soup to feed the stage-coach passengers with.

SECOND WAITER. Very well, ma'am. [*Exit* SECOND WAITER, C. DOOR.

Enter THIRD WAITER, *running,* C. DOOR.

Now, Will.

THIRD WAITER (*coming down* L. H.). A strange gentleman in a gig, ma'am, wants a private sitting-room.

MRS. NOAKES. Much luggage, Will?

THIRD WAITER. One portmanteau, and a great-coat.

MRS. NOAKES. Oh! nonsense!—Tell him to go into the commercial room.

THIRD WAITER. I told him so, ma'am, but the Strange Gentleman says he *will* have a private apartment, and that it's as much as his life is worth, to sit in a public room.

MRS. NOAKES. As much as his life is worth?

THIRD WAITER. Yes, ma'am.—Gentleman says he doesn't care if it's a dark closet; but a private room of some kind he must and will have.

MRS. NOAKES. Very odd.—Did you ever see him before, Will?

THIRD WAITER. No, ma'am; he's quite a stranger here.—He's a wonderful man to talk, ma'am—keeps on like a steam engine. Here he is, ma'am.

STRANGE GENTLEMAN (*without*). Now don't tell me, because that's all gammon and nonsense; and gammoned I never was, and never will be, by any waiter that ever drew the breath of life, or a cork.—And just have the goodness to leave my portmanteau alone, because I can carry it very well myself; and show me a private room without further delay; for a private room I must and will have.—Damme, do you think I'm going to be murdered!—

Enter the three Waiters, C. DOOR—*they form down* L. H., *the* STRANGE GENTLEMAN *following, carrying his portmanteau and great-coat.*

There—this room will do capitally well. Quite the thing,— just the fit.—How are you, ma'am? I suppose you are the landlady of this place? Just order those very attentive young fellows out, will you, and I'll order dinner.

MRS. NOAKES *(to Waiters)*. You may leave the room.

STRANGE GENTLEMAN. Hear that?—You may leave the room. Make yourselves scarce. Evaporate—disappear—come.

[*Exeunt Waiters,* C. DOOR.

That's right. And now, madam, while we're talking over this important matter of dinner, I'll just secure us effectually against further intrusion. *(Bolts the door.)*

MRS. NOAKES. Lor, sir! Bolting the door, and *me* in the room!

STRANGE GENTLEMAN. Don't be afraid—I won't hurt you. I have no designs against you, my dear ma'am : but *I must be private.* *(Sits on the portmanteau,* R. H.*)*

MRS. NOAKES. Well, sir—I have no objection to break through our rules for once; but it is not our way, when we're full, to give private rooms to solitary gentlemen, who come in a gig, and bring only one portmanteau. You're quite a stranger *here*, sir. If I'm not mistaken, it's your first appearance in this house.

STRANGE GENTLEMEN. You're right, ma'am. It *is* my first, my very first—but not my last, I can tell you.

MRS. NOAKES. No?

STRANGE GENTLEMAN. No *(looking round him)*. I like the look of this place. Snug and comfortable—neat and lively. You'll very often find me at the St. James's Arms, I can tell you, ma'am.

MRS. NOAKES *(aside)*. A civil gentleman. Are you a stranger in this town, sir?

STRANGE GENTLEMAN. Stranger! Bless you, no. I have been here for many years past, in the season.

MRS. NOAKES. Indeed!

STRANGE GENTLEMAN. Oh, yes. Put up at the Royal Hotel regularly for a long time; but I was obliged to leave it at last.

MRS. NOAKES. I have heard a good many complaints of it.

STRANGE GENTLEMAN. O! terrible! such a noisy house.

MRS. NOAKES. Ah!

STRANGE GENTLEMAN. Shocking! Din, din, din—Drum, drum, drum, all night. Nothing but noise, glare, and nonsense. I bore it a long time for old acquaintance sake; but what do you think they did at last, ma'am?

MRS. NOAKES. I can't guess.

STRANGE GENTLEMAN. Turned the fine Old Assembly Room into a stable, and took to keeping horses. I tried that too, but I found I couldnt' stand it; so I came away, ma'am, and—and —here I am. (*Rises.*)

MRS. NOAKES. And I'll be bound to say, sir, that you will have no cause to complain of the exchange.

STRANGE GENTLEMAN. I'm sure not, ma'am; I know it—I feel it, already.

MRS. NOAKES. About dinner, sir; what would you like to take?

STRANGE GENTLEMAN. Let me see; will you be good enough to suggest something, ma'am?

MRS. NOAKES. Why, a broiled fowl and mushrooms is a very nice dish.

STRANGE GENTLEMAN. You are right, ma'am; a broiled fowl and mushrooms form a very delightful and harmless amusement, either for one or two persons. Broiled fowl and mushrooms let it be, ma'am.

MRS. NOAKES. In about an hour, I suppose, sir?

STRANGE GENTLEMAN. For the second time, ma'am, you have anticipated my feelings.

MRS. NOAKES. You'll want a bed to-night, I suppose, sir; perhaps you'd like to see it? Step this way, sir, and—(*going* L. H.).

STRANGE GENTLEMAN. No, no, never mind. (*Aside.*) This is a plot to get me out of the room. She's bribed by somebody who wants to identify me. I must be careful; I am exposed to nothing but artifice and stratagem. Never mind, ma'am, never mind.

MRS. NOAKES. If you'll give me your portmanteau, sir, the Boots will carry it into the next room for you.

STRANGE GENTLEMAN (*aside*). Here's diabolical ingenuity; she thinks it's got the name upon it. (*To her.*) I'm very much obliged to the Boots for his disinterested attention, ma'am, but with your kind permission this portmanteau will remain just exactly where it is; consequently, ma'am, (*with greath warmth*,) if the aforesaid Boots wishes to succeed in removing this portmanteau, he must previously remove *me*, ma'am, *me*; and it will take a *pair* of very stout Boots to do that, ma'am, I promise you.

MRS. NOAKES. Dear me, sir, you needn't fear for your portmanteau in this house; I dare say nobody wants it.

STRANGE GENTLEMAN. I hope not, ma'am, because in that case nobody will be disappointed. (*Aside.*) How she fixes her old eyes on me!

MRS. NOAKES (*aside*). I never saw such an extraordinary person in all my life. What can he be? (*Looks at him very hard.*)

[*Exit* MRS. NOAKES, C. DOOR.

STRANGE GENTLEMAN. She's gone at last! Now let me commune with my own dreadful thoughts, and reflect on the best means of escaping from my horrible position. (*Takes a letter from his pocket.*) Here's an illegal death-warrant; a pressing invitation to be slaughtered; a polite request just to step out and be killed, thrust into my hand by some disguised assassin in a dirty black calico jacket, the very instant I got out of the gig at the door. I know the hand; there's a ferocious recklessness in the cross to this 'T,' and a baleful malignity in the dot of that 'I,' which warns me that it comes from my desperate rival. (*Opens it, and reads.*) 'Mr. Horatio Tinkles'—that's him —'presents his compliments to his enemy'—that's me—'and requests the pleasure of his company tomorrow morning, under the clump of trees, on Corpse Common,'—Corpse Common! —'to which any of the town's people will direct him, and where he hopes to have the satisfaction of giving him his gruel.' —Giving him his gruel! Ironical cut-throat!—'His punctuality will be esteemed a personal favour, as it will save Mr. Tinkles the trouble and inconvenience of calling with a horsewhip in his pocket. Mr. Tinkles has ordered breakfast at the Royal for *one*. It is paid for. The individual who returns alive can eat it. Pistols—half-past five—precisely.'—Bloodthirsty miscreant! *The* individual who returns alive! I have seen him hit the painted man at the shooting-gallery regularly every time in his centre shirt plait, except when he varied the entertainments, by lodging the ball playfully in his left eye. Breakfast! I shall want nothing beyond the gruel. What's to be done?

11

Escape! I can't escape; concealment's of no use, he knows I am here. He has dodged me all the way from London, and will dodge me all the way to the residence of Miss Emily Brown, whom my respected, but swine-headed parents have picked out for my future wife. A pretty figure I should cut before the old people, whom I have never beheld more than once in my life, and Miss Emily Brown, whom I have never seen at all, if I went down there, pursued by this Salamander, who, I suppose, is her accepted lover! What is to be done? I can't go back again; father would be furious. What can be done? nothing! (*Sinks into a chair.*) I must undergo this fiery ordeal, and submit to be packed up, and carried back to my weeping parents, like an unfortunate buck, with a flat piece of lead in my head, and a brief epitaph on my breast, 'Killed on Wednesday morning.' No, I won't (*starting up, and walking about*). I won't submit to it; I'll accept the challenge, but first I'll write an anonymous letter to the local authorities, giving them information of this intended duel, and desiring them to place me under immediate restraint. That's feasible; on further consideration, it's capital. My character will be saved—I shall be bound over—he'll be bound over—I shall resume my journey —reach the house—marry the girl—pocket the fortune, and laugh at him. No time to be lost; it shall be done forthwith. (*Goes to table and writes.*) There; the challenge accepted, with a bold defiance, that'll look very brave when it comes to be printed. Now for the other. (*Writes.*) 'To the Mayor—Sir—A strange Gentleman at the St. James's Arms, whose name is unknown to the writer of this communication, is bent upon committing a rash and sanguinary act, at an early hour tomorrow morning. As you value human life, secure the amiable youth, without delay. Think, I implore you, sir, think what would be the feelings of those to whom he is nearest and dearest, if any mischance befall the interesting young man. Do not neglect this solemn warning; the number of his room is seventeen.' There—(*folding it up*). Now if I can find any one who will deliver it secretly.—

TOM SPARKS, *with a pair of boots in his hand, peeps in at the* C. D.

TOM. Are these here your'n?

STRANGE GENTLEMAN. No.

Tom. Oh! (*going back*).

Strange Gentleman. Hallo! stop, are you the Boots?

Tom (*still at the door*). I'm the head o' that branch o' the establishment. There's another man under me, as brushes the dirt
off and puts the blacking on. The fancy work's my department.
I do the polishing, nothing else.

Strange Gentleman. You are the upper Boots, then?

Tom. Yes, I'm the reg'lar; t'other one's only the deputy; top
boots and half boots, I calls us.

Strange Gentleman. You're a sharp fellow.

Tom. Ah! I'd better cut then (*going*).

Strange Gentleman. Don't hurry, Boots—don't hurry; I want
you. (*Rises, and comes forward, R. H.*)

Tom (*coming forward, L. H.*). Well!

Strange Gentleman. Can—can—you be secret, Boots?

Tom. That depends entirely on accompanying circumstances;—
see the point?

Strange Gentleman. I think I comprehend your meaning,
Boots. You insinuate that you could be secret (*putting his hand
in his pocket*) if you had—five shillings for instance—isn't that
it, Boots?

Tom. That's the line o' argument I should take up; but that an't
exactly my meaning.

Strange Gentleman. No!

Tom. No. A secret's a thing as is always a rising to one's lips. It
requires an astonishing weight to keep one on 'em down.

Strange Gentleman. Ah!

Tom. Yes; I don't think I could keep one snug—reg'lar snug,
you know——

Strange Gentleman. Yes, regularly snug, of course.

Tom. —If it had a less weight a-top on it, than ten shillins.

Strange Gentleman. You don't think three half-crowns would
do it?

Tom. It might, I won't say it wouldn't, but I couldn't warrant it.

Strange Gentleman. You could the other!

Tom. Yes.

Strange Gentleman. Then there it is. (*Gives him four half-
crowns.*) You see these letters?

Tom. Yes, I can manage that without my spectacles.

Strange Gentleman. Well; that's to be left at the Royal Hotel.

This, *this*, is an anonymous one; and I want it to be delivered at the Mayor's house, without his knowing from whom it came, or seeing who delivered it.

Tom (*taking the letter*). I say—you're a rum 'un, you are.

Strange Gentleman. Think so! Ha, ha! so are you.

Tom. Ay, but you're a rummer one than me.

Strange Gentleman. No, no, that's your modesty.

Tom. No it an't. I say, how vell you did them last hay-stacks. How do you contrive that ere now, if it's a fair question. Is it done with a pipe, or do you use them Lucifer boxes?

Strange Gentleman. Pipe—Lucifer boxes—hay-stacks! Why, what do you mean?

Tom (*looking cautiously round*). I know your name, old 'un.

Strange Gentleman. You know my name! (*Aside.*) Now how the devil has he got hold of that, I wonder!

Tom. Yes, I know it. It begins with a 'S.'

Strange Gentleman. Begins with an S!

Tom. And ends with a 'G' (*winking*). We've all heard talk of *Swing* down here.

Strange Gentleman. Heard talk of Swing! Here's a situation! Damme, d'ye think I'm a walking carbois of vitriol, and burn everything I touch?—Will you go upon the errand you're paid for?

Tom. Oh, I'm going—I'm going. It's nothing to me, you know; I don't care. I'll only just give these boots to the deputy, to take them to whoever they belong to, and then I'll pitch this here letter in at the Mayor's office-window, in no time.

Strange Gentleman. Will you be off?

Tom. Oh, I'm going, I'm going. Close, you knows, close!

[*Exit* Tom, c. door.

Strange Gentleman. In five minutes more the letter will be delivered; in another half hour, if the Mayor does his duty, I shall be in custody, and secure from the vengeance of this infuriated monster. I wonder whether they'll take me away? Egad! I may as well be provided with a clean shirt and a nightcap in case. Let's see, she said the next room was my bed-room, and as I have accepted the challenge, I may venture so far now. (*Shouldering the portmanteau.*) What a capital notion it is; there'll be all the correspondence in large letters, in the county paper, and my name figuring away in roman capitals, with a long story, how I was such a desperate dragon, and so bent upon fighting, that it took four constables to carry me to the Mayor, and one boy to carry my hat. It's a capital plan—must be done—the only way I have of escaping unpursued from this place, unless I could put myself in the General Post, and direct myself to a friend in town. And then it's a chance whether they'd take me in, being so much over weight.

[*Exit* STRANGE GENTLEMAN, *with portmanteau*, L. H.

MRS. NOAKES, *peeping in* C. DOOR, *then entering*.

MRS. NOAKES. This is the room, ladies, but the gentleman has stepped out somewhere, he won't be long, I dare say. Pray come in, Miss.

Enter MARY *and* FANNY WILSON, C. DOOR.

MARY (C.). This is the Strange Gentleman's apartment, is it?

MRS. NOAKES (R.). Yes, Miss; shall I see if I can find him, ladies, and tell him you are here?

MARY. No; we should prefer waiting till he returns, if you please.

MRS. NOAKES. Very well, ma'am. He'll be back directly, I dare say; for it's very near his dinner time.

[*Exit* MRS. NOAKES, C. DOOR.

MARY. Come, Fanny, dear; don't give way to these feelings of depression. Take pattern by me—I feel the absurdity of our situation acutely; but you see that I keep up, nevertheless.

FANNY. It is easy for you to do so. *Your* situation is neither so embarrassing, nor so painful a one as mine.

MARY. Well, my dear, it *may* not be, certainly; but the circumstances which render it less so are, I own, somewhat incomprehensible to me. My harebrained, mad-cap swain, John Johnson, implores me to leave my guardian's house, and accompany him on an expedition to Gretna Green. I with immense reluctance and after considerable pressing——

FANNY. Yield a very willing consent.

MARY. Well, we won't quarrel about terms; at all events I *do* consent. He bears me off, and when we get exactly half-way, discovers that his money is all gone, and that we must stop at this Inn, until he can procure a remittance from London, by post. I think, my dear, you'll own that *this* is rather an embarrassing position.

15

FANNY. Compare it with mine. Taking advantage of your flight, I send express to *my* admirer, Charles Tomkins, to say that I have accompanied you; first, because I should have been miserable if left behind with a peevish old man alone; secondly, because I thought it proper that your sister should accompany you——

MARY. And, thirdly, because you knew that he would immediately comply with this indirect assent to his entreaties of three months' duration, and follow you without delay, on the same errand. Eh, my dear?

FANNY. It by no means follows that such was my intention, or that I knew he would pursue such a course, but supposing he *has* done so; supposing this Strange Gentleman should be himself——

MARY. *Supposing!*—Why, you know it is. You told him not to disclose his name, on any account; and the *Strange Gentleman* is not a very common travelling name, I should imagine; besides the hasty note, in which he said he should join you here.

FANNY. Well, granted that it is he. In what a situation am I placed. You tell me, for the first time, that *my* violent intended must on no account be beheld by *your* violent intended, just now, because of some old quarrel between them, of long standing, which has never been adjusted to this day. What an appearance this will have! How am I to explain it, or relate your present situation? I should sink into the earth with shame and confusion.

MARY. Leave it to me. It arises from my heedlessness. I will take it all upon myself, and see him alone. But tell me, my dear— as you got up this love affair with so much secrecy and expedition during the four months you spent at Aunt Martha's, I have never yet seen Mr Tomkins, you know. Is he so very handsome?

FANNY. See him, and judge for yourself.

MARY. Well, I will; and you may retire, till I have paved the way for your appearance. But just assist me first, dear, in making a little noise to attract his attention, if he really be in the next room, or I may wait here all day.

DUET—*At end of which exit* FANNY, C. DOOR. MARY *retires up*
R. H.

Enter STRANGE GENTLEMAN, L. H.

STRANGE GENTLEMAN. There; now with a clean shirt in one pocket and a night-cap in the other, I'm ready to be carried magnanimously to my dungeon in the cause of love.

MARY (*aside*). He says, he's ready to be carried magnanimously to a dungeon in the cause of love. I thought it was Mr. Tomkins! Hem! (*Coming down* L. H.)

STRANGE GENTLEMAN (*seeing her*). Hallo! Who's this! Not a disguised peace officer in petticoats. Beg your pardon, ma'am. (*Advancing towards her.*) What—did—you——

MARY. Oh, Sir; I feel the delicacy of my situation.

STRANGE GENTLEMAN (*aside*). Feels the delicacy of her situation; Lord bless us, what's the matter! Permit me to offer you a seat, ma'am, if you're in a delicate situation. (*He places chairs; they sit.*)

MARY. You are very good, Sir. You are surprised to see me here, Sir?

STRANGE GENTLEMAN. No, no, at least not very; rather, perhaps —rather. (*Aside.*) Never was more astonished in all my life!

MARY (*aside*). His politeness, and the extraordinary tale I have to tell him, overpower me. I must summon up courage. Hem!

STRANGE GENTLEMAN. Hem!

MARY. Sir!

STRANGE GENTLEMAN. Ma'am!

MARY. You have arrived at this house in pursuit of a young lady, if I mistake not?

STRANGE GENTLEMAN. You are quite right, ma'am. (*Aside.*) Mysterious female!

MARY. If you *are* the gentleman I'm in search of, you wrote a hasty note a short time since, stating that you would be found here this afternoon.

STRANGE GENTLEMAN (*drawing back his chair*). I—I—wrote a note, ma'am!

MARY. You need keep nothing secret from me, Sir. I know all.

STRANGE GENTLEMAN (*aside*). That villain, Boots, has betrayed me! Know all, ma'am?

MARY. Everything.

STRANGE GENTLEMAN (*aside*). It must be so. She's a constable's wife.

17

MARY. You *are* the writer of that letter, Sir? I think I am not mistaken.

STRANGE GENTLEMAN. You are not, ma'am; I confess I did write it. What was I to do, ma'am? Consider the situation in which I was placed.

MARY. In your situation, you had, as it appears to me, only one course to pursue.

STRANGE GENTLEMAN. You mean the course I adopted?

MARY. Undoubtedly.

STRANGE GENTLEMAN. I am very happy to hear you say so, though of course I should like it to be kept a secret.

MARY. Oh, of course.

STRANGE GENTLEMAN (*drawing his chair close to her, and speaking very softly*). Will you allow me to ask you, whether the constables are downstairs?

MARY (*surprised*). The constables!

STRANGE GENTLEMAN. Because if I am to be apprehended, I should like to have it over. I am quite ready, if it must be done.

MARY. No legal interference has been attempted. There is nothing to prevent your continuing your journey to-night.

STRANGE GENTLEMAN. But will not the other party follow?

MARY (*looking down*). The other party, I am compelled to inform you, is detained here by—by want of funds.

STRANGE GENTLEMAN (*starting up*). Detained here by want of funds! Hurrah! Hurrah! I have caged him at last. I'm revenged for all his blustering and bullying. This is a glorious triumph, ha, ha, ha! I have nailed him—nailed him to the spot!

MARY (*rising indignantly*). This exulting over a fallen foe, Sir, is mean and pitiful. In my presence, too, it is an additional insult.

STRANGE GENTLEMAN. Insult! I wouldn't insult you for the world, after the joyful intelligence you have brought me—I could hug you in my arms!—One kiss, my little constable's deputy. (*Seizing her.*)

MARY (*struggling with him*). Help! help!

Enter JOHN JOHNSON, C. DOOR.

JOHN. What the devil do I see! (*Seizes* STRANGE GENTLEMAN *by the collar.*)

MARY (L. H.). John, and Mr. Tomkins, met together! They'll kill each other.—Here, help! help!

[*Exit* MARY, *running*, C. DOOR.

JOHN (*shaking him*). What do you mean by that, scoundrel?

STRANGE GENTLEMAN. Come, none of your nonsense—there's no harm done.

JOHN. No harm done.—How dare you offer to salute that lady?

STRANGE GENTLEMAN. What did you send her here for?

JOHN. *I* send her here!

STRANGE GENTLEMAN. Yes, *you*; you gave her instructions, I suppose. (*Aside.*) Her husband, the constable, evidently.

JOHN. That lady, Sir, is attached to me.

STRANGE GENTLEMAN. Well, I know she is; and a very useful little person she must be, to be attached to anybody,—it's a pity she can't be legally sworn in.

JOHN. *Legally* sworn in! Sir, that is an insolent reflection upon the temporary embarrassment which prevents our taking the marriage vows. How dare you to insinuate——

STRANGE GENTLEMAN. Pooh! pooh!—don't talk about daring to insinuate; it doesn't become a man in your station of life——

JOHN. My station of life!

STRANGE GENTLEMAN. But as you have managed this matter very quietly, and say you're in temporary embarrassment—here— here's five shillings for you. (*Offers it.*)

JOHN. Five shillings! (*Raises his cane.*)

STRANGE GENTLEMAN (*flourishing a chair*). Keep off, sir!

Enter MARY, TOM SPARKS, *and two Waiters.*

MARY. Separate them, or there'll be murder! (TOM *clasps* STRANGE GENTLEMAN *round the waist—the Waiters seize* JOHN JOHNSON).

TOM. Come, none o' that 'ere, Mr. S. We don't let private rooms for such games as these.—If you want to try it on wery partickler, we don't mind making a ring for you in the yard, but you mustn't do it here.

JOHN. Let me get at him. Let me go; waiters—Mary, don't hold me. I insist on your letting me go.

STRANGE GENTLEMAN. Hold him fast.—Call yourself a *peace* officer, you prize-fighter!

19

JOHN (*struggling*). Let me go, I say!

STRANGE GENTLEMAN. Hold him fast! Hold him fast!

> [TOM *takes* STRANGE GENTLEMAN *off*, R. H. *Waiters take* JOHN *off*, L. H., MARY *following*.

SCENE II.—*Another Room in the Inn.*

Enter JULIA DOBBS *and* OVERTON, L. H.

JULIA. You seem surprised, Overton.

OVERTON. Surprised, Miss Dobbs! Well I may be, when, after seeing nothing of you for three years and more, you come down here without any previous notice, for the express purpose of running away—positively running away, with a young man. I am astonished, Miss Dobbs!

JULIA. You would have had better reason to be astonished if I had come down here with any notion of positively running away with an old one, Overton.

OVERTON. Old or young, it would matter little to me, if you had not conceived the preposterous idea of entangling me—*me*, an attorney, and mayor of the town, in so ridiculous a scheme.— Miss Dobbs, I can't do it.—I really cannot consent to mix myself up with such an affair.

JULIA. Very well, Overton, very well. You recollect that in the lifetime of that poor old dear, Mr. Woolley, who——

OVERTON. —Who would have married you, if he hadn't died; and who, as it was, left you his property, free from all incumbrances, the incumbrance of himself, as a husband, not being among the least.

JULIA. Well, you may recollect, that in the poor old dear's life-time, sundry advances of money were made to you, at my persuasion, which still remain unpaid. Oblige me by forwarding them to my agent in the course of the week, and I free you from any interference in this little matter. (*Crosses to* L. H *and is going.*)

OVERTON. Stay, Miss Dobbs, stay. As you say, we *are* old acquaintances, and there certainly *were* some small sums of money, which—which——

JULIA. Which certainly *are* still outstanding.

OVERTON. Just so, just so; and which, perhaps you would

be likely to forget, if you had a husband—eh, Miss Dobbs, eh?

JULIA. I have little doubt that I should. If I gained one through your assistance, indeed—I can safely say I should forget all about them.

OVERTON. My dear Miss Dobbs, we perfectly understand each other—Pray proceed.

JULIA. Well—dear Lord Peter——

OVERTON. That's the young man you're going to run away with, I presume?

JULIA. That's the young *nobleman* who's going to run away with me, Mr. Overton.

OVERTON. Yes, just so.—I beg your pardon—pray go on.

JULIA. Dear Lord Peter is young and wild, and the fact is, his friends do not consider him very sagacious or strong-minded. To prevent their interference, our marriage is to be a secret one. In fact, he is stopping now at a friend's hunting seat in the neighbourhood; he is to join me here; and we are to be married at Gretna.

OVERTON. Just so.—A matter, as it seems to me, which you can conclude without my interference.

JULIA. Wait an instant. To avoid suspicion, and prevent our being recognised and followed, I settled with him that you should give out in this house that he was a lunatic, and that I—his aunt—was going to convey him in a chaise, to-night, to a private asylum at Berwick. I have ordered the chaise at half-past one in the morning. You can see him, and make our final arrangements. It will avert all suspicion, if I have no communication with him, till we start. You can say to the people of the house that the sight of me makes him furious.

OVERTON. Where shall I find him?—Is he here?

JULIA. You know best.

OVERTON. I!

JULIA. I desired him, immediately on his arrival, to write you some mysterious nonsense, acquainting you with the number of his room.

OVERTON (*producing a letter*). Dear me, he has arrived, Miss Dobbs.

JULIA. No!

OVERTON. Yes—see here—a most mysterious and extraordinary

21

composition, which was thrown in at my office window this morning, and which I could make neither head nor tail of. Is that his handwriting? (*Giving her the letter.*)

JULIA (*taking letter*). I never saw it more than once, but I know he writes very large and straggling.—(*Looks at letter.*) Ha, ha, ha! This is capital, isn't it?

OVERTON. Excellent!—Ha, ha, ha!—So mysterious!

JULIA. Ha, ha, ha!—So very good.—'Rash act.'

OVERTON. Yes. Ha, ha!

JULIA. 'Interesting young man.'

OVERTON. Yes.—Very good.

JULIA. 'Amiable youth!'

OVERTON. Capital!

JULIA. 'Solemn warning!'

OVERTON. Yes.—That's best of all. (*They both laugh.*)

JULIA. Number seventeen, he says. See him at once, that's a good creature. (*Returning the letter.*)

OVERTON (*taking letter*). I will. (*He crosses to* L. H. *and rings a bell.*)

Enter WAITER, L. H.

Who is there in number seventeen, waiter?

WAITER. Number seventeen, sir?—Oh!—the strange gentleman, sir.

OVERTON. Show me the room.   [*Exit* WAITER, L. H. (*Looking at* JULIA, *and pointing to the letter.*) 'The Strange Gentleman.'—Ha, ha, ha! Very good—very good indeed—Excellent notion! (*They both laugh.*)   [*Exeunt severally.*

SCENE III.—*Same as the first.—A small table, with wine, dessert, and lights on it,* R. H. *of* C. DOOR; *two chairs.*

STRANGE GENTLEMAN *discovered seated at table.*

STRANGE GENTLEMAN. 'The other party is detained here, by want of funds.' Ha, ha, ha! I can finish my wine at my leisure, order my gig when I please, and drive on to Brown's in perfect security. I'll drink the other party's good health, and long may he be detained here. (*Fills a glass.*) Ha, ha, ha! The other party; and long may he—(*A knock at* C. DOOR.) Hallo! I hope *this* isn't the other party. Talk of the—(*A knock at* C. DOOR.)

Well—(*setting down his glass*)—this is the most extraordinary private room that was ever invented. I am continually disturbed by unaccountable knockings. (*A gentle tap at* C. DOOR.) There's another; that was a gentle rap—a persuasive tap— like a friend's fore-finger on one's coat-sleeve. It *can't* be Tinkles with the gruel.—Come in.

OVERTON *peeping in at* C. DOOR.

OVERTON. Are you alone, my Lord?

STRANGE GENTLEMAN (*amazed*). Eh!

OVERTON. Are you alone, my Lord?

STRANGE GENTLEMAN. My Lord!

OVERTON (*stepping in, and closing the door*). You are right, sir, we cannot be too cautious, for we do not know who may be within hearing. You are very right, sir.

STRANGE GENTLEMAN (*rising from table, and coming forward,* R. H.). It strikes me, sir, that you are very wrong.

OVERTON. Very good, very good; I like this caution; it shows me you are wide awake.

STRANGE GENTLEMAN. Wide awake!—damme, I begin to think I am fast asleep, and have been for the last two hours.

OVERTON (*whispering*). I—am—the mayor.

STRANGE GENTLEMAN (*in the same tone*). Oh!

OVERTON. This is your letter? (*Shows it;* STRANGE GENTLEMAN *nods assent solemnly.*) It will be necessary for you to leave here to-night, at half-past one o'clock, in a postchaise and four; and the higher you bribe the postboys to drive at their utmost speed, the better.

STRANGE GENTLEMAN. You don't say so?

OVERTON. I do indeed. You are not safe from pursuit here.

STRANGE GENTLEMAN. Bless my soul, can such dreadful things happen in a civilised community, Mr. Mayor?

OVERTON. It certainly does at first sight appear rather a hard case that people cannot marry whom they please, without being hunted down in this way.

STRANGE GENTLEMAN. To be sure. To be hunted down, and killed as if one was game, you know.

OVERTON. Certainly; and you *an't* game, you know.

STRANGE GENTLEMAN. Of course not. But can't you prevent it? can't you save me by the interposition of your power?

23

OVERTON. My power can do nothing in such a case.

STRANGE GENTLEMAN. Can't it, though?

OVERTON. Nothing whatever.

STRANGE GENTLEMAN. I never heard of such dreadful revenge, never! Mr. Mayor, I am a victim, I am the unhappy victim of parental obstinacy.

OVERTON. Oh, no; don't say that. You may escape yet.

STRANGE GENTLEMAN (*grasping his hand*). Do you think I may? Do you think I may, Mr. Mayor?

OVERTON. Certainly! certainly! I have little doubt of it, if you manage properly.

STRANGE GENTLEMAN. I thought I *was* managing properly. I understood the other party was detained here, by want of funds.

OVERTON. Want of funds!—There's no want of funds in that quarter, I can tell you.

STRANGE GENTLEMAN. An't there, though?

OVERTON. Bless you, no. Three thousand a year!—But who told you there was a want of funds?

STRANGE GENTLEMAN. Why, she did.

OVERTON. *She!* you *have* seen her then? She told me you had not.

STRANGE GENTLEMAN. Nonsense; don't believe her. She was in this very room half an hour ago.

OVERTON. Then I must have misunderstood her, and you must have misunderstood her too.—But to return to business. Don't you think it would keep up appearances if I had you put under some restraint.

STRANGE GENTLEMAN. I think it would. I am very much obliged to you. (*Aside.*) This regard for my character in an utter stranger, and in a Mayor too, is quite affecting.

OVERTON. I'll send somebody up, to mount guard over you.

STRANGE GENTLEMAN. Thank 'ee, my dear friend, thank 'ee.

OVERTON. And if you make a little resistance, when we take you upstairs to your bedroom, or away in the chaise, it will be keeping up the character, you know.

STRANGE GENTLEMAN. To be sure.—So it will.—I'll do it.

OVERTON. Very well, then. I shall see your Lordship again by and by.—For the present, my Lord, good evening. (*Going.*)

STRANGE GENTLEMAN. Lord!—Lordship!—Mr. Mayor!

OVERTON. Eh?—Oh!—I see. (*Comes forward.*) Practising the lunatic, my Lord. Ah, very good—very vacant look indeed.—Admirable, my Lord, admirable!—I say, my Lord—(*pointing to letter*)—'Amiable youth!'—'Interesting young man.'—'Strange Gentleman.'—Eh? Ha, ha, ha! Knowing trick indeed, my Lord, very! [*Exit* OVERTON, C. D.

STRANGE GENTLEMAN. That Mayor is either in the very last stage of mystified intoxication, or in the most hopeless state of incurable insanity.—I have no doubt of it. A little touched here (*tapping his forehead*). Never mind, he is sufficiently sane to understand my business at all events. (*Goes to table and takes a glass.*) Poor fellow!—I'll drink his health, and speedy recovery. (*A knock at* C. DOOR.) It is a most extraordinary thing, now, that every time I propose a toast to myself, some confounded fellow raps at that door, as if he were receiving it with the utmost enthusiasm. Private room!—I might as well be sitting behind the little shutter of a Two-penny Post Office, where all the letters put in were to be post-paid. (*A knock at* C. DOOR.) Perhaps it's the guard! I shall feel a great deal safer if it is. Come in. (*He has brought a chair forward, and sits* L. H.)

Enter TOM SPARKS, C. DOOR, *very slowly, with an enormous stick. He closes the door, and, after looking at the* STRANGE GENTLEMAN *very steadily, brings a chair down* L. H., *and sits opposite him.*

STRANGE GENTLEMAN. Are you sent by the mayor of this place, to mount guard over me?

TOM. Yes, yes.—It's all right.

STRANGE GENTLEMAN (*aside*). It's all right—I'm safe. (*To* TOM, *with affected indignation.*) Now mind, I have been insulted by receiving this challenge, and I want to fight the man who gave it me. I protest against being kept here. I denounce this treatment as an outrage.

TOM. Ay, ay. Anything you please—poor creature; don't put yourself in a passion. It'll only make you worse. (*Whistles*).

STRANGE GENTLEMAN. This is most extraordinary behaviour.—I don't understand it.—What d'ye mean by behaving in this manner? (*Rising.*)

TOM (*aside*). He's a getting wiolent. I must frighten him with a

25

steady look.—I say, young fellow, do you see this here eye? (*Staring at him, and pointing at his own eye.*)

STRANGE GENTLEMAN (*aside*). Do I see his eye!—What can he mean by glaring upon me, with that large round optic!—Ha! a terrible light flashes upon me.—He thought I was 'Swing' this morning. It was an insane delusion.—That eye is an insane eye.—He's a madman!

TOM. Madman! Damme, I think he is a madman with a wengeance.

STRANGE GENTLEMAN. He acknowledges it. He is sensible of his misfortune!—Go away—leave the room instantly, and tell them to send somebody else.—Go away!

TOM. Oh, you unhappy lunatic!

STRANGE GENTLEMAN. What a dreadful situation!—I shall be attacked, strangled, smothered, and mangled, by a madman! Where's the bell?

TOM (*advancing and brandishing his stick*). Leave that 'ere bell alone—leave that 'ere bell alone—and come here!

STRANGE GENTLEMAN. Certainly, Mr. Boots, certainly.—He's going to strangle me. (*Going towards table.*) Let me pour you out a glass of wine, Mr. Boots—pray do! (*Aside.*) If he said 'Yes,' I'd throw the decanter at his temple.

TOM. None o' your nonsense.—Sit down there. (*Forces him into a chair,* L. H.) I'll sit here. (*Opposite him,* R. H.) Look me full in the face, and I won't hurt you. Move hand, foot, or eye, and you'll never want to move either of 'em again.

STRANGE GENTLEMAN. I'm paralysed with terror.

TOM. Ha! (*raising his stick in a threatening attitude*).

STRANGE GENTLEMAN. I'm dumb, Mr. Boots—dumb, sir.

They sit gazing intently on each other; TOM *with the stick raised, as the Act Drop slowly descends.*

END OF ACT FIRST

———

ACT II

SCENE I.—*The same as* SCENE III, ACT I.

TOM SPARKS *discovered in the same attitude watching the* STRANGE GENTLEMAN, *who has fallen asleep with his head over the back of his Chair.*

TOM. He's asleep; poor unhappy wretch! How very mad he looks with his mouth wide open and his eyes shut! (STRANGE GENTLEMAN *snores*.) Ah! there's a wacant snore; no meaning in it at all. I cou'd ha' told he was out of his senses from the very tone of it. (*He snores again*.) That's a wery insane snore. I should say he was melancholy mad from the sound of it.

Enter, through C. DOOR, OVERTON, MRS. NOAKES, *a Chamber-maid, and two Waiters;* MRS. NOAKES *with a warming-pan, the Maid with a light.* STRANGE GENTLEMAN *starts up, greatly exhausted.*

TOM (*starting up in* C.). Hallo!—Hallo! keep quiet, young fellow. Keep quiet!

STRANGE GENTLEMAN (L. H.). Out of the way, you savage maniac. Mr. Mayor (*crossing to him,* R. H., the person you sent to keep guard over me is a madman, sir. What do you mean by shutting me up with a madman?—what do you mean, sir, I ask?

OVERTON, R. H. C. (*aside to* STRANGE GENTLEMAN). Bravo! bravo! very good indeed—excellent!

STRANGE GENTLEMAN. Excellent, sir!—It's horrible!—The bare recollection of what I have endured, makes me shudder, down to my very toe-nails.

MRS. NOAKES (R. H.). Poor dear!—Mad people always think other people mad.

STRANGE GENTLEMAN. Poor dear! Ma'am! What the devil do you mean by 'Poor dear'? How dare you have a madman here, ma'am, to assault and terrify the visitors to your establishment?

MRS. NOAKES. Ah! terrify indeed! I'll never have another, to please anybody, you may depend upon that, Mr. Overton. (*To* STRANGE GENTLEMAN.) There, there.—Don't exert yourself, there's a dear.

STRANGE GENTLEMAN (c.). Exert myself!—Damme! it's a mercy I have any life left to exert myself with. It's a special miracle, ma'am, that my existence has not long ago fallen a sacrifice to that sanguinary monster in the leather smalls.

OVERTON, R. C. (*aside to* STRANGE GENTLEMAN). I never saw any passion more real in my life. Keep it up, it's an admirable joke.

STRANGE GENTLEMAN. Joke!—joke!—Peril a precious life, and call it a joke,—you, a man with a sleek head and a broad-brimmed hat, who ought to know better, calling it a joke.—Are you mad too, sir,—are you mad? (*Confronting* OVERTON.)

TOM, L. H. (*very loud*). Keep your hands off. Would you murder the wery mayor, himself, you mis-rable being?

STRANGE GENTLEMAN. Mr. Mayor, I call upon you to issue your warrant for the instant confinement of that one-eyed Orson in some place of security.

OVERTON (*aside, advancing a little*). He reminds me that he had better be removed to his bedroom. He is right.—Waiters, carry the gentleman upstairs.—Boots, you will continue to watch him in his bedroom.

STRANGE GENTLEMAN. *He* continue!—What, am I to be boxed up again with this infuriated animal, and killed off, when he has done playing with me?—I won't go—I won't go—help there, help! (*The Waiters cross from* R. H. *to behind him.*)

Enter JOHN JOHNSON *hastily,* C. DOOR.

JOHN (*coming forward* L. H.). What on earth is the meaning of this dreadful outcry, which disturbs the whole house?

MRS. NOAKES. Don't be alarmed, sir, I beg.—They're only going to carry an unfortunate gentleman, as is out of his senses, to his bedroom.

STRANGE GENTLEMAN, C. (*to* JOHN). Constable—constable—do your duty—apprehend these persons—every one of them. Do you hear, officer, do you hear?—(*The Waiters seize him by the arms.*)—Here—here—you see this. You've seen the assault committed. Take them into custody—off with them.

MRS. NOAKES. Poor creature!—He thinks you are a constable, sir.

JOHN. Unfortunate man! It is the second time to-day that he has been the victim of this strange delusion.

STRANGE GENTLEMAN (*breaking from Waiters and going to*

John). L. H. Unfortunate man!—What, do *you* think I am mad?

John. Poor fellow! His hopeless condition is pitiable indeed. (*Goes up.*)

Strange Gentleman (*returning to* c.). They're all mad!—Every one of 'em!

Mrs. Noakes. Come now, come to bed—there's a dear young man, do.

Strange Gentleman. Who are you, you shameless old ghost, standing there before company, with a large warming-pan, and asking me to come to bed?—Are *you* mad?

Mrs. Noakes. Oh! he's getting shocking now. Take him away. —Take him away.

Overton. Ah, you had better remove him to his bedroom at once. (*The Waiters take him up by the feet and shoulders.*)

Strange Gentleman. Mind, if I survive this, I'll bring an action of false imprisonment against every one of you. Mark my words—especially against that villainous old mayor.—Mind, I'll do it! (*They bear him off, struggling and talking—the others crowding round, and assisting.*)

Overton (*following*). How well he does it! [*Exeunt* L. H. 1*st* E.

Enter a Waiter, showing in Charles Tomkins *in a travelling coat,* c. door.

Waiter (L. H.). This room is disengaged now, sir. There *was* a gentleman in it, but he has just left it.

Charles. Very well, this will do. I may want a bed here to-night, perhaps, waiter.

Waiter. Yes, sir.—Shall I take your card to the bar, sir?

Charles. My card!—No, never mind.

Waiter. No name, sir?

Charles. No—it doesn't matter.

Waiter (*aside, as going out*). *Another* Strange Gentleman!
[*Exit Waiter,* c. door.

Charles. Ah!—(*Takes off coat.*)—The sun and dust on this long ride have been almost suffocating. I wonder whether Fanny has arrived? If she has—the sooner we start forward on our journey further North the better. Let me see; she would be accompanied by her sister, she said in her note—and they would both be on the look-out for me. Then the best

29

thing I can do is to ask no questions, for the present at all events, and to be on the look-out for them. (*Looking towards* c. DOOR.) Why here she comes, walking slowly down the long passage, straight towards this room—she can't have seen me yet.—Poor girl, how melancholy she looks! I'll keep in the background for an instant, and give her a joyful surprise. (*He goes up* R. H.)

Enter FANNY, C. DOOR.

FANNY (L. H.). Was ever unhappy girl placed in so dreadful a situation!—Friendless, and almost alone, in a strange place— my dear, dear Charles a victim to an attack of mental derangement, and I unable to avow my interest in him, or express my anxious sympathy and solicitude for his sufferings! I cannot bear this dreadful torture of agonising suspense. I must and will see him, let the cost be what it may. (*She is going* L. H.)

CHARLES (*coming forward* R. H.). Hist! Fanny!

FANNY (*starting and repressing a scream*). Ch—Charles—here in this room!

CHARLES. Bodily present, my dear, in this very room. My darling Fanny, let me strain you to my bosom. (*Advancing.*)

FANNY (*shrinking back*). N—n—no, dearest Charles, no, not now. —(*Aside.*)—How flushed he is!

CHARLES. No!—Fanny, this cold reception is a very different one to what I looked forward to meeting with, from you.

FANNY (*advancing, and offering the tip of her finger*). N—n—no —not cold, Charles; not cold. I do not mean it to be so, in-deed.—How is your head, now dear?

CHARLES. How is my head! After days and weeks of suspense and anxiety, when half our dangerous journey is gained, and I meet you here, to bear you whither you can be made mine for life, you greet me with the tip of your longest finger, and inquire after my head,—Fanny, what can you mean?

FANNY. You—you have startled me rather, Charles.—I thought you had gone to bed.

CHARLES. Gone to bed!—Why I have but this moment arrived.

FANNY (*aside*). Poor, poor Charles!

CHARLES. Miss Wilson, what am I to——

FANNY. No, no; pray, pray, do not suffer yourself to be excited——

30

CHARLES. Suffer myself to be excited!—Can I possibly avoid it?
can I do aught but wonder at this extraordinary and sudden
change in your whole demeanour?—Excited! But five minutes
since, I arrived here, brimful of the hope and expectation
which had buoyed up my spirits during my long journey.
I find you cold, reserved, and embarrassed—everything but
what I expected to find you—and then you tell me not to be
excited.

FANNY (*aside*). He is wandering again. The fever is evidently upon
him.

CHARLES. This altered manner and ill-disguised confusion all
convince me of what you would fain conceal. Miss Wilson,
you repent of your former determination, and love another!

FANNY. Poor fellow!

CHARLES. Poor fellow!—What, am I pitied?

FANNY. Oh, Charles, do not give way to this. Consider how much
depends upon your being composed.

CHARLES. I see how much depends upon my being composed,
ma'am—well, very well.—A husband depends upon it, ma'am.
Your new lover is in this house, and if he overhears my reproaches he will become suspicious of the woman who has
jilted *another*, and may jilt *him*. That's it, madam—a great
deal depends, as you say, upon my being composed.—A great
deal, ma'am.

FANNY. Alas! these are indeed the ravings of frenzy!

CHARLES. Upon my word, ma'am, you must form a very modest
estimate of your own power, if you imagine that disappointment has impaired my senses. Ha, ha, ha!—I am delighted. I
am delighted to have escaped you, ma'am. I am glad, ma'am
—damn'd glad! (*Kicks a chair over.*)

FANNY (*aside*). I must call for assistance. He grows more incoherent and furious every instant.

CHARLES. I leave you, ma'am.—I am unwilling to interrupt the
tender *tête-à-tête* with the other gentleman, to which you are,
no doubt, anxiously looking forward.—To you I have no more
to say. To *him* I must beg to offer a few rather unexpected
congratulations on his approaching marriage.

[*Exit* CHARLES *hastily,* C. DOOR.

FANNY. Alas! it is but too true. His senses have entirely left him.

[*Exit* L. H.

SCENE SECOND AND LAST.—*A Gallery in the Inn, leading to the Bedrooms. Four doors in the Flat, and one at each of the upper Entrances, numbered from 20 to 25, beginning at the* R. H. *A pair of boots at the door of 23.*

Enter Chambermaid with two lights; and CHARLES TOMKINS, R. H. 1*st* E.

MAID. This is your room, sir, No. 21. (*Opening the door.*)

CHARLES. Very well. Call me at seven in the morning.

MAID. Yes, sir. (*Gives him a light, and*

[*Exit Chambermaid,* R. H. 1*st* E.

CHARLES. And at nine, if I can previously obtain a few words of explanation with this unknown rival, I will just return to the place from whence I came, in the same coach that brought me down here. I wonder who he is and where he sleeps. (*Looking round.*) I have a lurking suspicion of those boots. (*Pointing to No.* 23.) They are an ill-looking, underhanded sort of pair, and an undefinable instinct tells me that they have clothed the feet of the rascal I am in search of. Besides myself, the owner of those ugly articles is the only person who has yet come up to bed. I will keep my eyes open for half an hour or so; and my ears too.

[*Exit* CHARLES *into No.* 21.

Enter R. H. 1*st* E. MRS. NOAKES *with two lights, followed by* MARY *and* FANNY.

MRS. NOAKES. Take care of the last step, ladies. This way, ma'am, if you please. No. 20 is your room, ladies : nice large double-bedded room, with coals and a rushlight.

FANNY, R. H. (*aside to* MARY). I must ask which is his room. I cannot rest unless I know he has at length sunk into the slumber he so much needs. (*Crosses to* MRS. NOAKES, *who is* L. H.) Which is the room in which the Strange Gentleman sleeps?

MRS. NOAKES. No. 23, ma'am. There's his boots outside the door. Don't be frightened of him, ladies. He's very quiet now, and our Boots is a watching him.

FANNY. Oh, no—we are not afraid of him. (*Aside.*) Poor Charles!

MRS. NOAKES (*going to door No.* 20, *which is* 3*rd* E. R. H.). This way, if you please; you'll find everything very comfortable, and there's a bell-rope at the head of the bed, if you want anything in the morning. Good night, ladies.

As MARY *and* FANNY *pass* MRS. NOAKES, FANNY *takes a light.*

[*Exeunt* FANNY *and* MARY *into No.* 20.

MRS. NOAKES (*tapping at No.* 23). Tom—Tom—

Enter TOM *from No.* 23.

TOM (*coming forward*, L. H.). Is that you, missis?

MRS. NOAKES (R. H.). Yes—How's the Strange Gentleman, Tom?

TOM. He was wery boisterous half an hour ago, but I punched his head a little, and now he's uncommon comfortable. He's fallen asleep, but his snores is still wery incoherent.

MRS. NOAKES. Mind you take care of him, Tom. They'll take him away in half an hour's time. It's very nearly one o'clock now.

TOM. I'll pay ev'ry possible attention to him. If he offers to call out, I shall whop him again.   [*Exit* TOM *into No.* 23.

MRS. NOAKES (*looking off* R. H.). This way, ma'am, if you please. Up these stairs.

Enter JULIA DOBBS *with a light*, R. H. 1*st* E.

JULIA. Which did you say was the room in which I could arrange my dress for travelling?

MRS. NOAKES. No. 22, ma'am; the next room to your nephew's. Poor dear—he's fallen asleep, ma'am, and I dare say you'll be able to take him away very quietly by and by.

JULIA (*aside*). Not so quietly as you imagine, if he plays his part half as well as Overton reports he does. (*To* MRS. NOAKES.) Thank you.—For the present, good night.

[*Exit* JULIA *into No.* 22.

MRS. NOAKES. Wish you good night, ma'am. There.—Now I think I may go downstairs again, and see if Mr. Overton wants any more negus. Why who's this? (*Looking off* R. H.) Oh, I forgot—No. 24 an't a-bed yet.—It's him.

Enter JOHN JOHNSON *with a light*, R. H. 1*st* E.

MRS. NOAKES. No. 24, sir, if you please.

JOHN. Yes, yes, I know. The same room I slept in last night. (*Crossing* L. H.)

33

MRS. NOAKES. Yes, sir.—Wish you good night, sir.

[*Exit* MRS. NOAKES, R. H. 1*st* E.

JOHN. Good night, ma'am. The same room I slept in last night, indeed, and the same room I may sleep in to-morrow night, and the next night, and the night after that, and just as many more nights as I can get credit here, unless this remittance arrives. I could raise the money to prosecute my journey without difficulty were I on the spot; but my confounded thoughtless liberality to the post-boys has left me absolutely penniless. Well, we shall see what to-morrow brings forth. (*He goes into No. 24, but immediately returns and places his boots outside his room door, leaving it ajar.*)   [*Exit* JOHN *into No.* 24.

CHARLES *peeping from No.* 21, *and putting out his boots.*

CHARLES. There's another pair of boots. Now I wonder which of these two fellows is the man. I can't help thinking it's No. 23. —Hallo! (*He goes in and closes his door.*)

The door of No. 20 *opens;* FANNY *comes out with a light in a night shade. No.* 23 *opens. She retires into No.* 20.

Enter TOM SPARKS, *with a stable lantern from No.* 23.

TOM (*closing the door gently*). Fast asleep still. I may as vell go my rounds, and glean for the deputy. (*Pulls out a piece of chalk from his pocket, and takes up boots from No.* 23.) Twenty-three. It's difficult to tell what a fellow is ven he han't got his senses, but I think this here twenty-three's a timorious faint-hearted genus. (*Examines the boots.*) You want new soleing, No. 23. (*Goes to No.* 24, *takes up boots and looks at them.*) Hallo! here's a *bust*: and there's been a piece put on in the corner.—I must let my missis know. The bill's always doubtful ven there's any mending. (*Goes to No.* 21, *takes up boots.*) French calf Vellingtons.—All's right here. These here French calves always comes it strong—light vines, and all that 'ere. (*Looking round.*) Werry happy to see there an't no high-lows —they never drinks nothing but gin-and-vater. Them and the cloth boots is the vurst customers an inn has.—The cloth boots is always obstemious, only drinks sherry vine and vater, and never eats no suppers. (*He chalks the No. of the room on each pair of boots as he takes them up.*) Lucky for you, my French calves, that you an't done with the patent polish, or you'd ha' been witrioled in no time. I don't like to put oil of witriol on a well-made pair of boots; but ven they're rubbed with that 'ere polish, it must be done, or the profession's ruined.

[*Exit* TOM *with boots*, R. H. 1*st* E.

Enter FANNY *from No.* 20, *with light as before.*

FANNY. I tremble at the idea of going into his room, but surely at a moment like this, when he is left to be attended by rude and uninterested strangers, the strict rules of propriety which regulate our ordinary proceedings may be dispensed with. I will but satisfy myself that he sleeps, and has those comforts which his melancholy situation demands, and return immediately. (*Goes to No.* 23, *and knocks.*)

CHARLES TOMKINS *peeping from No.* 21.

CHARLES. I'll swear I heard a knock.—A woman! Fanny Wilson —and at that door at this hour of the night!

FANNY *comes forward.*

Why what an ass I must have been ever to have loved that girl. —It *is* No. 23, though.—I'll throttle him presently. The next room door open—I'll watch there. (*He crosses to No.* 24, *and goes in.*)

FANNY *returns to No.* 23, *and knocks—the door opens and the* STRANGE GENTLEMAN *appears, night-cap on his head and a light in his hand.*—FANNY *screams and runs back into No.* 20.

STRANGE GENTLEMAN (*coming forward*). Well, of all the wonderful and extraordinary houses that ever did exist, this particular tenement is the most extraordinary. I've got rid of the madman at last—and it's almost time for that vile old mayor to remove me. But where?—I'm lost, bewildered, confused, and actually begin to think I am mad. Half these things I've seen to-day must be visions of fancy—they never could have really happened. No, no, I'm clearly mad!—I've not the least doubt of it now. I've caught it from that horrid Boots. He has inoculated the whole establishment. We're all mad together.— (*Looking off* R. H.) Lights coming upstairs!—Some more lunatics. [*Exit* STRANGE GENTLEMAN *in No.* 23.

Enter R. H. 1*st* E. OVERTON *with a cloak*, MRS. NOAKES, TOM SPARKS *with lantern, and three Waiters with lights. The Waiters range up* R. H. *side.* TOM *is in* R. H. *corner and* MRS. NOAKES *next to him.*

OVERTON. Remain there till I call for your assistance. (*Goes up to No.* 23 *and knocks.*)

Enter STRANGE GENTLEMAN *from No.* 23.

Now, the chaise is ready.—Muffle yourself up in this cloak. (*Puts it on the* STRANGE GENTLEMAN.—*They come forward.*)

STRANGE GENTLEMAN (L. H.). Yes.

OVERTON (C.). Make a little noise when we take you away, you know.

STRANGE GENTLEMAN. Yes—yes.—I say, what a queer room this is of mine. Somebody has been tapping at the wall for the last half hour, like a whole forest of woodpeckers.

OVERTON. Don't you know who that was?

STRANGE GENTLEMAN. No.

OVERTON. The other party.

STRANGE GENTLEMAN (*alarmed*). The other party!

OVERTON. To be sure.—The other party is going with you.

STRANGE GENTLEMAN. Going with me!—In the same chaise!

OVERTON. Of course.—Hush! (*Goes to No.* 22. *Knocks.*)

Enter JULIA DOBBS *from No.* 22, *wrapped up in a large cloak.*

Look here! (*Bringing her forward.* JULIA *is next to* MRS. NOAKES.)

STRANGE GENTLEMAN (*starting into* L. H. CORNER). I won't go—I won't go. This is a plot—a conspiracy. I won't go, I tell you. I shall be assassinated.—I shall be murdered!

FANNY *and* MARY *appear at No.* 20, JOHNSON *and* TOMKINS *at* 24.

JOHN (*at the door*). I told you he was mad.

CHARLES (*at the door*). I see—I see—poor fellow!

JULIA (*crossing to* STRANGE GENTLEMAN *and taking his arm*). Come, dear, come.

MRS. NOAKES. Yes, do go, there's a good soul. Go with your affectionate aunt.

STRANGE GENTLEMAN (*breaking from her*). My affectionate aunt!

JULIA *returns to her former position.*

TOM. He don't deserve no affection. I niver see such an unfectionate fellow to his relations.

STRANGE GENTLEMAN (L. H.). Take that wretch away, and smother him between two feather beds. Take him away, and make a sandwich of him directly.

JULIA (*to* OVERTON, *who is in* C.). What voice was that?—It was not Lord Peter's. (*Throwing off her cloak.*)

OVERTON. Nonsense—nonsense.—Look at him. (*Pulls cloak off* STRANGE GENTLEMAN.)

STRANGE GENTLEMAN (*turning round*). A woman!

JULIA. A stranger!

OVERTON. A stranger! What, an't he your husband that is to— your mad nephew, I mean?

JULIA. No!

ALL. No!

STRANGE GENTLEMAN. No!—no, I'll be damned if I am. I an't anybody's nephew.—My aunt's dead, and I never had an uncle.

MRS. NOAKES. And an't he mad, ma'am?

JULIA. No.

STRANGE GENTLEMAN. Oh, I'm *not* mad.—I was mistaken just now.

OVERTON. And isn't he going away with you?

JULIA. No.

MARY (*coming forward* R. H., *next to* MRS. NOAKES). And isn't his name Tomkins?

STRANGE GENTLEMAN (*very loud*). No!

(*All these questions and answers should be very rapid.* JOHNSON *and* TOMKINS *advance to the ladies, and they all retire up.*)

MRS. NOAKES. What *is* his name? (*Producing a letter.*) It an't Mr. Walker Trott, is it? (*She advances a little towards him.*)

STRANGE GENTLEMAN. Something so remarkably like it, ma'am, that, with your permission, I'll open that epistle. (*Taking letter*).

All go up, but JULIA *and* STRANGE GENTLEMAN.

(*Opening letter.*) Tinkle's hand. (*Reads.*) 'The challenge was a *ruse*. By this time I shall have been united at Gretna Green to the charming Emily Brown.'—Then, through a horror of duels, I have lost a wife!

JULIA (R. H. *with her handkerchief to her eyes*). And through Lord Peters' negligence, I have lost a husband!

STRANGE GENTLEMAN. Eh! (*Regards her a moment, then beckons* OVERTON, *who comes forward*, L. H.) I say, didn't you say something about three thousand a year this morning?

OVERTON. I did.

STRANGE GENTLEMAN. You alluded to that party? (*Nodding towards* JULIA.)

OVERTON. I did.

STRANGE GENTLEMAN. Hem! (*Puts* OVERTON *back*.) Permit me, ma'am (*going to her*), to sympathise most respectfully with your deep distress.

JULIA. Oh, sir! your kindness penetrates to my very heart.

STRANGE GENTLEMAN (*aside*). Penetrates to her heart!—It's taking the right direction.—If I understand your sorrowing murmur, ma'am, you contemplated taking a destined husband away with you, in the chaise at the door?

JULIA. Oh! sir,—spare my feelings—I did.—The horses were ordered and paid for; and everything was ready. (*Weeps*.)

STRANGE GENTLEMAN (*aside*). She weeps.——Expensive thing, posting, ma'am.

JULIA. Very, sir.

STRANGE GENTLEMAN. Eighteen-pence a mile, ma'am, not including the boys.

JULIA. Yes, sir.

STRANGE GENTLEMAN. *You've* lost a husband, ma'am—*I* have lost a wife.—Marriages are made above—I'm quite certain ours is booked.—Pity to have all this expense for nothing—let's go together.

JULIA (*drying her eyes*). The suddenness of this proposal, sir——

STRANGE GENTLEMAN. Requires a sudden answer, ma'am.—You don't say no—you mean yes. Permit me to—(*kisses her*).—All right! Old one (*to* OVERTON, *who comes down* L. H.), I've done it.—Mrs. Noakes (*she comes down* R. H.), don't countermand the chaise.—We're off directly.

CHARLES (*who with* FANNY *comes down* L. H. C.). So are we.

JOHN (*who with* MARY *comes down* R. H. C.). So are we, thanks to a negotiated loan, and an explanation as hasty as the quarrel that gave rise to it.

STRANGE GENTLEMAN. Three post-chaises and four, on to Gretna, directly.   [*Exeunt Waiters*, R. H. 1*st* E.

I say—we'll stop here as we come back?

JOHN *and* CHARLES. Certainly.

STRANGE GENTLEMAN. But before I go, as I fear I have given a great deal of trouble here to-night—permit me to inquire whether you will view my mistakes and perils with an indulgent eye, and consent to receive '*The Strange Gentleman*' again to-morrow.

IS SHE HIS WIFE?
OR, SOMETHING SINGULAR!

A Comic Burletta

IN ONE ACT
[1837]

'As an exquisite embodiment of the poet's visions, and a realisation of human intellectuality, gilding with refulgent light our dreamy moments, and laying open a new and magic world before the mental eye, the drama is gone, perfectly gone,' said Mr. Curdle.

'What man is there, now living, who can present before us all those changing and prismatic colours with which the character of Hamlet is invested?' exclaimed Mrs. Curdle.

'What man indeed—upon the stage,' said Mr. Curdle, with a small reservation in favour of himself. 'Hamlet! Pooh! ridiculous! Hamlet is gone, perfectly gone.'

DRAMATIS PERSONÆ

AT ST. JAMES'S THEATRE, MARCH 6, 1837

ALFRED LOVETOWN, ESQ.	MR. FORESTER.
MR. PETER LIMBURY	MR. GARDNER.
FELIX TAPKINS, ESQ. (*formerly of the India House, Leadenhall Street, and Prospect Place, Poplar; but now of the Rustic Lodge, near Reading*) . .	MR. HARLEY.
JOHN (*servant to Lovetown*)	————
MRS. LOVETOWN	MISS ALLISON.
MRS. PETER LIMBURY	MADAME SALA.

IS SHE HIS WIFE?

OR, SOMETHING SINGULAR!

SCENE I.—*A Room opening into a Garden. A Table laid for Breakfast; Chairs, etc.* MR. *and* MRS. LOVETOWN, C., *discovered at Breakfast,* R. H. *The former in a dressing-gown and slippers, reading a newspaper. A Screen on one side.*

LOVETOWN (L. H. *of table, yawning*). Another cup of tea, my dear,—O Lord!

MRS. LOVETOWN (R. H. *of table*). I wish, Alfred, you would endeavour to assume a more cheerful appearance in your wife's society. If you are perpetually yawning and complaining of *ennui* a few months after marriage, what am I to suppose you'll become in a few years? It really is very odd of you.

LOVETOWN. Not at all odd, my dear, not the least in the world; it would be a great deal more odd if I were not. The fact is, my love, I'm tired of the country; green fields, and blooming hedges, and feathered songsters, are fine things to talk about and read about and write about; but I candidly confess that I prefer paved street, area railings and dustman's bells, after all.

MRS. LOVETOWN. How often have you told me that, blessed with my love, you could live contented and happy in a desert?

LOVETOWN (*reading*). 'Artful imposter!'

MRS. LOVETOWN. Have you not over and over again said that fortune and personal attractions were secondary considerations with you? That you loved me for those virtues which, while they gave additional lustre to public life, would adorn and sweeten retirement?

LOVETOWN (*reading*). 'Soothing syrup!'

MRS. LOVETOWN. You complain of the tedious sameness of a country life. Was it not you yourself who first proposed our residing permanently in the country? Did you not say that I should then have an ample sphere in which to exercise those

43

charitable feelings which I have so often evinced, by selling at those benevolent fancy fairs?

LOVETOWN (*reading*). 'Humane man-traps!'

MRS. LOVETOWN. He pays no attention to me,—Alfred dear,——

LOVETOWN (*stamping his foot*). Yes, my life.

MRS. LOVETOWN. Have you heard what I have just been saying, dear?

LOVETOWN. Yes, love.

MRS. LOVETOWN. And what can you say in reply?

LOVETOWN. Why, really, my dear, you've said it so often before in the course of the last six weeks, that I think it quite unnecessary to say anything more about it. (*Reads.*) 'The learned judge delivered a brief but impressive summary of the unhappy man's trial.'

MRS. LOVETOWN (*aside*). I could bear anything but this neglect. He evidently does not care for me.

LOVETOWN (*aside*). I could put with anything rather than these constant altercations and little petty quarrels. I repeat, my dear that I am very dull in this out-of-the-way villa—confoundedly dull, horridly dull.

MRS. LOVETOWN. And *I* repeat that if you took any pleasure in your wife's society, or felt for her as you once professed to feel, you would have no cause to make such a complaint.

LOVETOWN. If I did not know you to be one of the sweetest creatures in existence, my dear, I should be strongly disposed to say that you were a very close imitation of an aggravating female.

MRS. LOVETOWN. That's very curious, my dear, for I declare that if I hadn't known *you* to be such an exquisite, good-tempered, attentive husband, I should have mistaken you for a very great brute.

LOVETOWN. My dear, you're offensive.

MRS. LOVETOWN. My love, you're intolerable. (*They turn their chairs back to back.*)

MR. FELIX TAPKINS *sings without.*

'The wife around her husband throws
    Her arms to make him stay;
"My dear, it rains, it hails, it blows,
    And you cannot hunt to-day."

44

But a hunting we will go,
And a hunting we will go,—wo—wo—wo!
And a hunting we will go.'

MRS. LOVETOWN. There's that dear, good-natured creature, Mr. Tapkins,—do you ever hear *him* complain of the tediousness of a country life? Light-hearted creature,—his lively disposition and rich flow of spirits are wonderful, even to me. (*Rising.*)

LOVETOWN. They need not be a matter of astonishment to anybody, my dear,—he's a bachelor.

MR. FELIX TAPKINS *appears at window*, L. H.

TAPKINS. Ha, ha! How are you both?—Here's a morning! Bless my heart alive, *what* a morning! I've been gardening ever since five o'clock, and the flowers have been actually growing before my very eyes. The London Pride is sweeping everything before it, and the stalks are half as high again as they were yesterday. They're all run up like so many tailors' bills, after that heavy dew of last night broke down half my rosebuds with the weight of its own moisture,—something like a dew that!—reg'lar *doo*, eh?—come, that's not so bad for a before-dinner one.

LOVETOWN. Ah, you happy dog, Felix!

TAPKINS. Happy! of course I am,—Felix by name, Felix by nature—what the deuce should I be unhappy for, or anybody be unhappy for? What's the use of it, that's the point?

MRS. LOVETOWN. Have you finished your improvements yet, Mr. Tapkins?

TAPKINS. At Rustic Lodge? (*She nods assent.*) Bless your heart and soul! you never saw such a place,—cardboard chimneys, Grecian balconies,—Gothic parapets, thatched roof.

MRS. LOVETOWN. Indeed!

TAPKINS. Lord bless you, yes,—green verandah, with ivy twining round the pillars.

MRS. LOVETOWN. How very rural!

TAPKINS. Rural, my dear Mrs. Lovetown! delightful! The French windows, too! Such an improvement!

MRS. LOVETOWN. I should think they were!

TAPKINS. Yes, *I* should think they were. Why, on a fine summer's evening the frogs hop off the grass-plot into the very sitting-room.

45

MRS. LOVETOWN. Dear me!

TAPKINS. Bless you, yes! Something like the country,—quite a little Eden. Why, when I'm smoking under the verandah, after a shower of rain, the black beetles fall into my brandy-and-water.

MR. *and* MRS. LOVETOWN. No!—Ha! ha! ha!

TAPKINS. Yes. And I take 'em out again with the teaspoon, and lay bets with myself which of them will run away the quickest. Ha! ha! ha! (*They all laugh.*) Then the stable, too. Why, in Rustic Lodge the stables are close to the dining-room window.

LOVETOWN. No!

TAPKINS. Yes. The horse can't cough but I hear him. There's compactness. Nothing like the cottage style of architecture for comfort, my boy. By the bye, I have left the new horse at your garden-gate this moment.

MRS. LOVETOWN. The new horse!

TAPKINS. The new horse! Splendid fellow,—such action! Puts out its feet like a rocking-horse, and carries its tail like a hat-peg. Come and see him.

LOVETOWN (*laughing*). I can't deny you anything.

TAPKINS. No, that's what they all say, especially the—eh! (*Nodding and winking.*)

LOVETOWN. Ha! ha! ha!

MRS. LOVETOWN. Ha! ha! ha! I'm afraid you're a very bad man, Mr. Tapkins; I'm afraid you're a shocking man, Mr. Tapkins.

TAPKINS. Think so? No, I don't know,—not worse than other people similarly situated. Bachelors, my dear Mrs. Lovetown, bachelors—eh! old fellow? (*Winking to* LOVETOWN.)

LOVETOWN. Certainly, certainly.

TAPKINS. *We* know—eh? (*They all laugh.*) By the bye, talking of bachelors puts me in mind of Rustic Lodge, and talking of Rustic Lodge puts me in mind of what I came here for. You must come and see me this afternoon. Little Peter Limbury and his wife are coming.

MRS. LOVETOWN. I detest that man.

LOVETOWN. The wife is supportable, my dear.

TAPKINS. To be sure, so she is. You'll come, and that's enough. Now come and see the horse.

46

LOVETOWN. Give me three minutes to put on my coat and boots, and I'll join you. I won't be three minutes.

[*Exit* LOVETOWN, R. H.

TAPKINS. Look sharp, look sharp!—Mrs. Lovetown, will you excuse me one moment? (*Crosses to* L.; *calling off.*) Jim,— these fellows never know how to manage horses,—walk him gently up and down,—throw the stirrups over the saddle to show the people that his master's coming, and if anybody asks what the fine animal's pedigree is, and who he belongs to, say he's the property of Mr. Felix Tapkins of Rustic Lodge, near Reading, and that he's the celebrated horse who ought to have won the Newmarket Cup last year, only he didn't.

[*Exit* TAPKINS.

MRS. LOVETOWN. My mind is made up,—I can bear Alfred's coldness and insensibility no longer, and come what may I will endeavour to remove it. From the knowledge I have of his disposition I am convinced that the only mode of doing so will be by rousing his jealousy and wounding his vanity. This thoughtless creature will be a very good instrument for my scheme. He plumes himself on his gallantry, has no very small share of vanity, and is easily led. I see him crossing the garden. (*She brings a chair hastily forward and sits* R. H.)

Enter FELIX TAPKINS, L. H. *window.*

TAPKINS (*singing*). 'My dear, it rains, it hails, it blows'——

MRS. LOVETOWN (*tragically*). Would that I had never beheld him!

TAPKINS (*aside*). Hallo! She's talking about her husband. I knew by their manner there had been a quarrel, when I came in this morning.

MRS. LOVETOWN. So fascinating, and yet so insensible to the tenderest of passions as not to see how devotedly I love him.

TAPKINS (*aside*). I thought so.

MRS. LOVETOWN. That he should still remain unmarried is to me extraordinary.

TAPKINS. Um!

MRS. LOVETOWN. He ought to have married long since.

TAPKINS (*aside*). Eh! Why, they aren't married!—'ought to have married long since.'—I rather think he ought.

MRS. LOVETOWN. And, though I am the wife of another,——

47

TAPKINS (*aside*). Wife of another!

MRS. LOVETOWN. Still, I grieve to say that I cannot be blind to his extraordinary merits.

TAPKINS. Why, he's run away with somebody else's wife! The villain!—I must let her know I'm in the room, or there's no telling what I may hear next. (*Coughs.*)

MRS. LOVETOWN (*starting up in affected confusion*). Mr. Tapkins! (*They sit.*) Bring your chair nearer. I fear, Mr. Tapkins, that I have been unconsciously giving utterance to what was passing in my mind. I trust you have not overheard my confession of the weakness of my heart.

TAPKINS. No—no—not more than a word or two.

MRS. LOVETOWN. That agitated manner convinces me that you have heard more than you are willing to confess. Then why—why should I seek to conceal from you—that though I esteem my husband, I—I—love—another?

TAPKINS. I heard you mention that little circumstance.

MRS. LOVETOWN. Oh! (*Sighs.*)

TAPKINS (*aside*). What the deuce is she Oh-ing at? She looks at me as if I were Lovetown himself.

MRS. LOVETOWN (*putting her hand on his shoulder with a languishing air*). Does my selection meet with your approbation?

TAPKINS (*slowly*). It doesn't.

MRS. LOVETOWN. No!

TAPKINS. Decidedly not. (*Aside.*) I'll cut that Lovetown out, and offer myself. Hem! Mrs. Lovetown.

MRS. LOVETOWN. Yes, Mr. Tapkins.

TAPKINS. I know an individual——

MRS. LOVETOWN. Ah! an individual!

TAPKINS. An individual,—I may, perhaps, venture to say an estimable individual,—who for the last three months has been constantly in your society, who never yet had courage to disclose his passion, but who burns to throw himself at your feet. Oh! (*Aside.*) I'll try an Oh or two now,—Oh! (*Sighs.*) That's a capital Oh!

MRS. LOVETOWN (*aside*). He must have misunderstood me before, for he is evidently speaking of himself. Is the gentleman you speak of handsome, Mr. Tapkins?

TAPKINS. He is generally considered remarkably so.

MRS. LOVETOWN. Is he tall?

48

TAPKINS. About the height of the Apollo Belvidere.

MRS. LOVETOWN. Is he stout?

TAPKINS. Of nearly the same dimensions as the gentleman I have just named.

MRS. His figure is——

TAPKINS. Quite a model.

MRS. LOVETOWN. And he is——

TAPKINS. Myself. (*Throws himself on his knees and seizes her hand.*)

Enter LOVETOWN, R H.

TAPKINS *immediately pretends to be diligently looking for something on the floor.*

MRS. LOVETOWN. Pray don't trouble yourself. I'll find it. Dear me! how could I lose it?

LOVETOWN. What have you lost, love? I should almost imagine that you had lost yourself, and that our friend Mr. Tapkins here had just found you.

TAPKINS (*aside*). Ah! you always will have your joke,—funny dog! funny dog! Bless my heart and soul, there's that immortal horse standing outside all this time! He'll catch his death of cold! Come and see him at once,—come—come.

LOVETOWN. No. I can't see him to-day. I had forgotten. I've letters to write,—business to transact,—I'm engaged.

TAPKINS (*to* MRS. LOVETOWN). Oh! if he's engaged, you know, we'd better not interrupt him.

MRS. LOVETOWN. Oh! certainly! Not by any means.

TAPKINS (*taking her arm*). Good-bye, old fellow.

LOVETOWN (*seating himself at table*). Oh!—good-bye.

TAPKINS (*going*). Take care of yourself. I'll take care of Mrs. L.
[*Exeunt* TAPKINS *and* MRS. LOVETOWN, C.

LOVETOWN. What the deuce does that fellow mean by laying such emphasis on Mrs. L.? What's my wife to him, or he to my wife? Very extraordinary! I can hardly believe that even if he had the treachery to make any advances, she would encourage such a preposterous intrigue. (*Walks to and fro.*) She spoke in his praise at breakfast-time, though,—and they have gone away together to see that confounded horse. But stop, I must keep a sharp eye upon them this afternoon, without appearing to do so. I would not appear unnecessarily suspicious for the

49

world. Dissembling in such a case, though, is difficult—very difficult.

Enter a Servant, L. H.

SERVANT. Mr. and Mrs. Peter Limbury.

LOVETOWN. Desire them to walk in.   [*Exit Servant*, L. H.
A lucky visit! it furnishes me with a hint. This Mrs. Limbury is a vain, conceited woman, ready to receive the attentions of anybody who feigns admiration for her, partly to gratify herself, and partly to annoy the jealous little husband whom she keeps under such strict control. If I pay particular attention to *her*, I shall lull my wife and that scoundrel Tapkins into a false security, and have better opportunities of observation. They are here.

Enter MR. *and* MRS. LIMBURY, L. H.

LOVETOWN. My dear Mrs. Limbury. (*Crosses to* C.)

LIMBURY. Eh?

LOVETOWN (*not regarding him*). How charming—how delightful—how divine you look to-day.

LIMBURY (*aside*). Dear Mrs. Limbury,—charming,—divine and beautiful look to-day! They are smiling at each other,—he squeezes her hand. I see how it is. I always thought he paid her too much attention.

LOVETOWN. Sit down,—sit down.

(LOVETOWN *places the chairs so as to sit between them, which* LIMBURY *in vain endeavours to prevent.*)

MRS. LIMBURY. Peter and I called as we passed in our little pony-chaise, to inquire whether we should have the pleasure of seeing you at Tapkins's this afternoon.

LOVETOWN. Is it possible you can ask such a question? Do you think I could stay away?

MRS. LIMBURY. Dear Mr. Lovetown! (*Aside.*) How polite,—he's quite struck with me.

LIMBURY (*aside*). Wretched miscreant! a regular assignation before my very face.

LOVETOWN (*to* MRS. LIMBURY). Do you know I entertained some apprehensions—some dreadful fears—that you might not be there.

LIMBURY. Fears that we mightn't be there? Of course we shall be there.

MRS. LIMBURY. Now don't talk, Peter.

LOVETOWN. I thought it just possible, you know, that you might not be agreeable——

MRS. LIMBURY. O, Peter is always agreeable to anything that is agreeable to me. Aren't you, Peter?

LIMBURY. Yes, dearest. (*Aside*.) Agreeable to anything that's agreeable to her! O Lor'!

MRS. LIMBURY. By the bye, Mr. Lovetown, how do you like this bonnet?

LOVETOWN. O, beautiful!

LIMBURY (*aside*). I must change the subject. Do you know, Mr. Lovetown, I have often thought, and it has frequently occurred to me—when——

MRS. LIMBURY. Now don't talk, Peter. (*To* LOVETOWN.) The colour is so bright, is it not?

LOVETOWN. It might appear so elsewhere, but the brightness of those eyes casts it quite into shade.

MRS. LIMBURY. I know you are a connoisseur in ladies' dresses: how do you like those shoes?

LIMBURY (*aside*). Her shoes! What will she ask his opinion of next?

LOVETOWN. O, like the bonnet, you deprive them of their fair chance of admiration. That small and elegant foot engrosses all the attention which the shoes might otherwise attract. That taper ankle, too——

LIMBURY (*aside*). Her taper ankle! My bosom swells with the rage of an ogre. Mr. Lovetown,—I——

MRS. LIMBURY. Now, pray do not talk so, Limbury. You've put Mr. Lovetown out as it is.

LIMBURY (*aside*). Put him out! I wish I could put him out, Mrs. Limbury. I must.

Enter Servant, hastily.

SERVANT. I beg your pardon, sir, but the bay pony has got his hind leg over the traces, and he's kicking the chaise to pieces!

LIMBURY. Kicking the *new* chaise to pieces!

LOVETOWN. Kicking the new chaise to pieces! The bay pony! Limbury, my dear fellow, fly to the spot! (*Pushing him out.*)

LIMBURY. But, Mr. Lovetown, I——

MRS. LIMBURY. Oh! he'll kick somebody's brains out, if Peter don't go to him.

LIMBURY. But perhaps he'll kick my brains out if I do go to him.

LOVETOWN. Never mind, don't lose an instant,—not a moment. (*Pushes him out, both talking together.*) [*Exit* LIMBURY. (*Aside.*) Now for it,—here's my wife. Dearest Mrs. Limbury— (*Kneels by her chair, and seizes her hand.*)

Enter MRS. LOVETOWN, C.

MRS. LOVETOWN (*aside*). Can I believe my eyes? (*Retires behind the screen.*)

MRS. LIMBURY. Mr. Lovetown!

LOVETOWN. Nay. Allow me in one hurried interview, which I have sought for in vain for weeks,—for months,—to say how devotedly, how ardently I love you. Suffer me to retain this hand in mine. Give me one ray of hope.

MRS. LIMBURY. Rise, I entreat you,—we shall be discovered.

LOVETOWN. Nay, I will not rise till you promise me that you will take an opportunity of detaching yourself from the rest of the company and meeting me alone in Tapkins's grounds this evening. I shall have no eyes, no ears for any one but yourself.

MRS. LIMBURY. Well,—well,—I will—I do——

LOVETOWN. Then I am blest indeed!

MRS. LIMBURY. I am so agitated. If Peter or Mrs. Lovetown— were to find me thus—I should betray all. I'll teach my husband to be jealous! (*Crosses to* L. H.) Let us walk round the garden.

LOVETOWN. With pleasure,—take my arm. Divine creature! (*Aside.*) I'm sure she is behind the screen. I saw her peeping. Come.

[*Exit* LOVETOWN *and* MRS. LIMBURY, L. H.

MRS. LOVETOWN (*coming forward*). Faithless man! His coldness and neglect are now too well explained. O Alfred! Alfred! how little did I think when I married you, six short months since, that I should be exposed to so much wretchedness! I begin to tremble at my own imprudence, and the situation in which it may place me; but it is now too late to recede. I must be firm. This day will either bring my project to the explanation I so much desire, or convince me of what I too much fear,—my husband's aversion. Can this woman's husband suspect their intimacy? If so, he may be able to prevent this assignation taking place. I will seek him instantly. If I can but meet him at once, he may prevent her going at all.

[*Exit* MRS. LOVETOWN, R. H.

Enter TAPKINS, L. H. *window.*

TAPKINS. This, certainly, is a most extraordinary affair. Not her partiality for me,—that's natural enough,—but the confession I overheard about her marriage to another. I have been thinking that, after such a discovery, it would be highly improper to allow Limbury and his wife to meet her without warning him of the fact. The best way will be to make him acquainted with the real state of the case. Then he must see the propriety of not bringing his wife to my house to-night. Ah! here he is. I'll make the awful disclosure at once, and petrify him.

Enter LIMBURY, L. H. *window.*

LIMBURY. That damned little bay pony is as bad as my wife. There's no curbing either of them; and as soon as I have got the traces of the one all right, I lose all traces of the other.

TAPKINS (R.). Peter!

LIMBURY (L.). Ah! Tapkins!

TAPKINS. Hush! Hush! (*Looking cautiously round.*) If you have a moment to spare, I've got something of great importance to communicate.

LIMBURY. Something of great importance, Mr. Tapkins! (*Aside.*) What can he mean? Can it relate to Mrs. Limbury? The thought is dreadful. You horrify me!

TAPKINS. You'll be more horrified presently. What I am about to tell you concerns yourself and your honour very materially; and I beg you to understand that I communicate it—in the strictest confidence.

LIMBURY. Myself and my honour! I shall dissolve into nothing with horrible anticipations!

TAPKINS (*in a low tone*). Have you ever observed anything remarkable about Lovetown's manner?

LIMBURY. Anything remarkable?

TAPKINS. Ay,—anything very odd, and rather unpleasant?

53

LIMBURY. Decidedly! No longer than half an hour ago,—in this very room, I observed something in his manner particularly odd and exceedingly unpleasant.

TAPKINS. To your feelings as a husband?

LIMBURY. Yes, my friend, yes, yes;—you know it all, I see!

TAPKINS. What! Do *you* know it?

LIMBURY. I'm afraid I do; but go on—go on.

TAPKINS (*aside*). How the deuce can he know anything about it? Well, this oddness arises from the peculiar nature of his connexion with—— You look very pale.

LIMBURY. No, no,—go on,—'connexion with——'

TAPKINS. A certain lady,—you know whom I mean.

LIMBURY. I do, I do! (*Aside.*) Disgrace and confusion! I'll kill her with a look! I'll wither her with scornful indignation! Mrs. Limbury!—viper!

TAPKINS (*whispering with caution*). They—aren't—married.

LIMBURY. *They* aren't married! *Who* aren't?

TAPKINS. Those two, to be sure!

LIMBURY. *Those* two! *What* two?

TAPKINS. Why them. And the worst of it is she's—she's married to somebody else.

LIMBURY. Well, of course I know that.

TAPKINS. You know it?

LIMBURY. Of course I do. Why, how you talk! Isn't she my wife?

TAPKINS. *Your* wife! Wretched bigamist! Mrs. Lovetown your wife?

LIMBURY. Mrs. Lovetown! What! Have you been talking of Mrs. Lovetown all this time? My dear friend! (*Embraces him.*) The revulsion of feeling is almost insupportable. I thought you were talking about Mrs. Limbury.

TAPKINS. No!

LIMBURY. Yes. Ha! ha! But I say, what a dreadful fellow this is —another man's wife! Gad, I think he wants to run away with every man's wife he sees. And Mrs. Lovetown, too—horrid!

TAPKINS. Shocking!

LIMBURY. I say, I oughtn't to allow Mrs. Limbury to associate with her, ought I?

TAPKINS. Precisely my idea. You had better induce your wife to stay away from my house to-night.

LIMBURY. I'm afraid I can't do that.

TAPKINS. What, has she any particular objection to staying away?

LIMBURY. She has a very strange inclination to go, and 'tis much the same; however, I'll make the best arrangement I can!

TAPKINS. Well, so be it. Of course I shall see *you*?

LIMBURY. Of course.

TAPKINS. Mind the secret,—close—close—you know, as a Cabinet Minister answering a question.

LIMBURY. You may rely upon me.

[*Exit* LIMBURY, L. H., TAPKINS, R. H.

SCENE II.—*A Conservatory on one side. A Summer-house on the other.*

Enter LOVETOWN *at* L. H.

LOVETOWN. So far so good. My wife has not dropped the slightest hint of having overheard the conversation between me and Mrs. Limbury; but she cannot conceal the impression it has made upon her mind, or the jealousy it has evidently excited in her breast. This is just as I wished. I made Mr. Peter Limbury's amiable helpmate promise to meet me here. I know that refuge for destitute reptiles (*pointing to summer-house*) is Tapkins's favourite haunt, and if he has any assignation with my wife, I have no doubt he will lead her to this place. A woman's coming down the walk. Mrs. Limbury, I suppose,—no, my wife, by all that's actionable. I must conceal myself here, even at the risk of a shower of black beetles, or a marching regiment of frogs. (*Goes into conservatory*, L. H.)

Enter MRS. LOVETOWN *from top*, L. H.

MRS. LOVETOWN. I cannot have been mistaken. I am certain I saw Alfred here; he must have secreted himself somewhere to avoid me. Can his assignation with Mrs. Limbury have been discovered? Mr. Limbury's behaviour to me just now was strange in the extreme; and after a variety of incoherent expressions he begged me to meet him here, on a subject, as he said, of great delicacy and importance to myself. Alas! I fear that my husband's neglect and unkindness are but too well

55

Enter MR. LIMBURY *at top*, L. H.

known. The injured little man approaches. I summon all my fortitude to bear the disclosure.

LIMBURY (*aside*). Now as I could not prevail on Mrs. Limbury to stay away, the only distressing alternative I have is to inform Mrs. Lovetown that I know her history, and to put it to her good feeling whether she hadn't better go.

LOVETOWN. (*peeping*). Limbury! what the deuce can that little wretch want here?

LIMBURY. I took the liberty, Mrs. Lovetown, of begging you to meet me in this retired spot, because the esteem I still entertain for you, and my regard for your feelings, induce me to prefer a private to a public disclosure.

LOVETOWN (*peeping*). 'Public disclosure!' what on earth is he talking about? I wish he'd speak a little louder.

MRS. LOVETOWN. I am sensible of your kindness, Mr. Limbury, and believe me most grateful for it. I am fully prepared to hear what you have to say.

LIMBURY. It is hardly necessary for me, I presume, to say, Mrs. Lovetown, that I have accidentally discovered the whole secret.

MRS. LOVETOWN. The whole secret, sir?

LOVETOWN (*peeping*). Whole secret! What secret?

LIMBURY. The whole secret, ma'am, of this disgraceful—I must call it disgraceful—and most abominable intrigue.

MRS. LOVETOWN (*aside*). My worst fears are realised,—my husband's neglect is occasioned by his love for another.

LOVETOWN (*peeping*). Abominable intrigue! My first suspicions are too well founded. He reproaches my wife with her infidelity, and she cannot deny it,—that villain Tapkins!

MRS. LOVETOWN (*weeping*). Cruel—cruel—Alfred!

LIMBURY. You may well call him cruel, unfortunate woman. His usage of you is indefensible, unmanly, scandalous.

MRS. LOVETOWN. It is. It is, indeed.

LIMBURY. It's very painful for me to express myself in such plain terms, Mrs. Lovetown; but allow me to say, as delicately as possible, that you should not endeavour to appear in society under such unusual and distressing circumstances.

MRS. LOVETOWN. Not appear in society! Why should I quit it?

LOVETOWN (*peeping*). Shameful woman!

56

LIMBURY. Is it possible you can ask such a question?

MRS. LOVETOWN. What should I do? Where can I go?

LIMBURY. Gain permission to return once again to your husband's roof.

MRS. LOVETOWN. My husband's roof?

LIMBURY. Yes, the roof of your husband, your wretched, unfortunate husband!

MRS. LOVETOWN. Never!

LIMBURY (*aside*). She's thoroughly hardened, steeped in vice beyond redemption. Mrs. Lovetown, as you reject my well-intentioned advice in this extraordinary manner, I am reduced to the painful necessity of expressing my hope that you will,— now pray don't think me unkind,—that you will never attempt to meet Mrs. Limbury more.

MRS. LOVETOWN. What! Can you suppose I am so utterly dead to every sense of feeling and propriety as to meet that person, —the destroyer of my peace and happiness,—the wretch who has ruined my hopes and blighted my prospects for ever? Ask your own heart, sir,—appeal to your own feelings. *You* are naturally indignant at her conduct. *You* would hold no further communication with her. Can you suppose, then, *I* would deign to do so? The mere supposition is an insult!

[*Exit* MRS. LOVETOWN *hastily at top*, L. H.

LIMBURY. What can all this mean? I am lost in a maze of astonishment, petrified at the boldness with which she braves it out. Eh! it's breaking upon me by degrees. I see it. What did she say? 'Destroyer of peace and happiness,—person—ruined hopes and blighted prospects—*her*.' I see it all. That atrocious Lovetown, that Don Juan multiplied by twenty, that unprecedented libertine, has seduced Mrs. Limbury from her allegiance to her lawful lord and master. He first of all runs away with the wife of another man, and he is no sooner tired of her, than he runs away with another wife of another man. I thirst for his destruction. I—(LOVETOWN *rushes from the conservatory and embraces* LIMBURY, *who disengages himself.*) Murderer of domestic happiness! behold your victim!

LOVETOWN. Alas! you speak but too truly. (*Covering his face with his hands.*) I am the victim.

LIMBURY. I speak but too truly!—He avows his own criminality. I shall throttle him. I know I shall. I feel it.

Enter MRS. LIMBURY *at back*, L. H.

MRS. LIMBURY (*aside*). My husband here! (*Goes into conservatory.*)

Enter TAPKINS *at back*, L. H.

TAPKINS (*aside*). Not here, and her husband with Limbury. I'll reconnoitre. (*Goes into summer-house,* R. H.)

LIMBURY. Lovetown, have you the boldness to look an honest man in the face?

LOVETOWN. O, spare me! I feel the situation in which I am placed acutely, deeply. Feel for me when I say that from that conservatory I overheard the greater part of what passed between you and Mrs. Lovetown.

LIMBURY. You did?

LOVETOWN. Need I say how highly I approve both of the language you used, and the advice you gave her?

LIMBURY. What! you want to get rid of her, do you?

LOVETOWN. Can you doubt it?

TAPKINS (*peeping*). Hallo! he wants to get rid of her. Queer!

LOVETOWN. Situated as I am, you know, I have no other resource, after what has passed. I must part from her.

MRS. LIMBURY (*peeping*). What can he mean?

LIMBURY (*aside*). I should certainly throttle him, were it not that the coolness with which he refers to the dreadful event paralyses me. Mr. Lovetown, look at me! Sir, consider the feelings of an indignant husband, sir!

LOVETOWN. Oh, I thank you for those words. Those strong expressions prove the unaffected interest you take in the matter.

LIMBURY. Unaffected interest! I shall go raving mad with passion and fury! Villain! Monster! To embrace the opportunity afforded him of being on a footing of friendship.

LOVETOWN. To take a mean advantage of his being a single man.

LIMBURY. To tamper with the sacred engagements of a married woman.

LOVETOWN. To place a married man in a disgraceful and humiliating situation.

LIMBURY. Scoundrel! Do you mock me to my face?

LOVETOWN. Mock *you*! What d'ye mean? Who the devil are you talking about?

LIMBURY. Talking about—*you*!

LOVETOWN. Me!

LIMBURY. Designing miscreant! Of whom do *you* speak?

LOVETOWN. Of whom should I speak but that scoundrel Tapkins?

TAPKINS (*coming forward*, R.). Me! What the devil do you mean by that?

LOVETOWN. Ha! (*Rushing at him, is held back by* LIMBURY.)

LIMBURY (*to* TAPKINS). Avoid him. Get out of his sight. He's raving mad with conscious villainy.

TAPKINS. What are you all playing at *I spy I* over my two acres of infant hay for?

LOVETOWN (*to* TAPKINS). How dare you tamper with the affections of Mrs. Lovetown?

TAPKINS. O, is that all? Ha! ha! (*Crosses to* C.)

LOVETOWN. All!

TAPKINS. Come, come, none of your nonsense.

LOVETOWN. Nonsense! Designate the best feelings of our nature nonsense!

TAPKINS. Pooh! pooh! Here, I know all about it.

LOVETOWN (*angrily*). And so do I, sir. And so do I.

TAPKINS. Of course you do. And you've managed very well to keep it quiet so long. But you're a deep fellow, by Jove! you're a deep fellow!

LOVETOWN. Now, mind! I restrain myself sufficiently to ask you once again before I knock you down, by what right dare you tamper with the affections of Mrs. Lovetown?

TAPKINS. Right! O, if you come to strict right, you know, nobody has a right but her husband.

LOVETOWN. And who is her husband? Who is her husband?

TAPKINS. Ah! to be sure, that's the question. Nobody that I know. I hope—poor fellow——

LOVETOWN. I'll bear these insults no longer! (*Rushes towards* TAPKINS. LIMBURY *interposes.* LOVETOWN *crosses to* R. H. *A scream is heard from the conservatory—a pause.*)

TAPKINS. Something singular among the plants! (*He goes into the conservatory and returns with* MRS. LIMBURY.) A flower that wouldn't come out of its own accord. I was obliged to force it. Tolerably full blown now, at all events.

LIMBURY. My wife! Traitoress! (*Crosses to* L. H.) Fly from my

59

presence! Quit my sight! Return to the conservatory with that
demon in a frock-coat!

Enter MRS. LOVETOWN *at top*, L. H., *and comes down* C.

TAPKINS. Hallo! Somebody else!

LOVETOWN (*aside*). My wife here!

MRS. LOVETOWN (*to* LIMBURY). I owe you some return for the
commiseration you expressed just now for my wretched situation. The best, the only one I can make you is, to entreat you
to refrain from committing any rash act, however excited you
may be, and to control the feelings of an injured husband.

TAPKINS. Injured husband! Decidedly singular!

LOVETOWN. The allusion of that lady I confess my utter inability
to understand. Mr. Limbury, to you an explanation is due,
and I make it more cheerfully, as my abstaining from doing
so might involve the character of your wife. Stung by the
attentions which I found Mrs. Lovetown had received from a
scoundrel present,——

TAPKINS (*aside*). That's me.

LOVETOWN. I—partly to obtain opportunities of watching her
closely, under an assumed mask of levity and carelessness, and
partly in the hope of awakening once again any dormant
feelings of affection that might still slumber in her breast,
affected a passion for your wife which I never felt, and to
which she never really responded. The second part of my
project, I regret to say, has failed. The first has succeeded but
too well.

LIMBURY. Can I believe my ears? But how came Mrs. Peter
Limbury to receive those attentions?

MRS. LIMBURY. Why, not because I liked them, of course, but to
assist Mr. Lovetown in his project, and to teach you the misery
of those jealous fears. Come here, you stupid little jealous
insinuating darling. (*They retire up* L. H., *she coaxing him.*)

TAPKINS (*aside*). It strikes me very forcibly that I have made a
slight mistake here, which is something particularly singular.
(*Turns up* R. H.)

MRS. LOVETOWN. Alfred, hear me! I am as innocent as yourself.
Your fancied neglect and coldness hurt my weak vanity, and
roused some foolish feelings of angry pride. In a moment of
irritation I resorted to some such retaliation as you have your-

self described. That I did so from motives as guiltless as your own I call Heaven to witness. That I repent my fault I solemnly assure you.

LOVETOWN. Is this possible?

TAPKINS. Very possible indeed! Believe your wife's assurance and my corroboration. Here, give and take is all fair, you know. Give me your hand and take your wife's. Here, Mr. and Mrs. L. (*To* LIMBURY.) Double L,—I call them. (*To* LOVETOWN.) Small italic and Roman capital. (*To* MR. *and* MRS. LIMBURY, *who come forward.*) Here, it's all arranged. The key to the whole matter is, that I've been mistaken, which is something singular. If I have made another mistake in calculating on *your* kind and lenient reception of our last half-hour's misunderstanding (*to the audience*), I shall have done something more singular still. Do you forbid me committing any more mistakes, or may I announce my intention of doing something singular again?

CURTAIN

THE LAMPLIGHTER

A Farce

IN ONE ACT
[1838]

Quite overcome by these dismal reflections, Mr. and Mrs.
Curdle sighed, and sat for some short time without speaking.
At length, the lady, turning to Miss Snevellicci, inquired what
play she proposed to have.

'Quite a new one,' said Miss Snevellicci, 'of which this
gentleman is the author, and in which he plays; being his first
appearance on any stage. Mr. Johnson is the gentleman's
name.'

'I hope you have preserved the unities, sir?' said Mr.
Curdle.

'The original piece is a French one,' said Nicholas. 'There
is abundance of incident, sprightly dialogue, strongly-marked
character——'

'——All unavailing without a strict observance of the unities,
sir,' returned Mr. Curdle. 'The unities of the drama, before
everything.'

DRAMATIS PERSONÆ

MR. STARGAZER.
MASTER GALILEO ISAAC NEWTON FLAMSTEAD STARGAZER (*his son*).
TOM GRIG (*the Lamplighter*).
MR. MOONEY (*an astrologer*).
SERVANT.
BETSY MARTIN.
EMMA STARGAZER.
FANNY BROWN.

THE LAMPLIGHTER

SCENE I.—*The Street, outside of* MR. STARGAZER'S *house. Two street Lamp-posts in front.*

TOM GRIG (*with ladder and lantern, singing as he enters*).
Day has gone down o'er the Baltic's proud bil-ler;
Evening has sigh'd, alas! to the lone wil-ler;
Night hurries on, night hurries on, earth and ocean to kiv-ver;
Rise, gentle moon, rise, gentle moon, and guide me to my——
That ain't a rhyme, that ain't—kiv-ver and lover! I ain't much of a poet; but if I couldn't make better verse than that, I'd undertake to be set fire to, and put up, instead of the lamp, before Alderman Waithman's obstacle in Fleet Street. Bil-ler, wil-ler, kiv-ver—shiver, obviously. That's what *I* call poetry. (*Sings.*)
Day has gone down o'er the Baltic's proud bil-ler—

(*During the previous speech he has been occupied in lighting one of the lamps. As he is about to light the other,* MR. STARGAZER *appears at window, with a telescope.*)

MR. STARGAZER (*after spying most intently at the clouds*). Holloa!
TOM (*on ladder*). Sir, to you! And holloa again, if you come to that.
MR. STARGAZER. Have you seen the comet?
TOM. What Comet—the Exeter Comet?
MR. STARGAZER. What comet? *The* comet—Halley's comet!
TOM. Nelson's you mean. I saw it coming out of the yard, not five minutes ago.
MR. STARGAZER. Could you distinguish anything of a tail?
TOM. Distinguish a tail? I believe you—four tails?
MR. STARGAZER. A comet with four tails; and all visible to the naked eye! Nonsense! it couldn't be.

65

TOM. You wouldn't say that again if you was down here, old bantam. (*Clock strikes five.*) You'll tell me next, I suppose, that that isn't five o'clock striking, eh?

MR. STARGAZER. Five o'clock—five o'clock! Five o'clock P.M. on the thirtieth day of November, one thousand eight hundred and thirty-eight! Stop till I come down—stop! Don't go away on any account—not a foot, not a step. (*Closes window.*)

TOM (*descending, and shouldering his ladder*). Stop! stop, to a lamplighter, with three hundred and seventy shops and a hundred and twenty private houses waiting to be set a light to! Stop, to a lamplighter!

As he is running off, enter MR. STARGAZER *from his house, hastily.*

MR. STARGAZER (*detaining him*). Not for your life!—not for your life! The thirtieth day of November, one thousand eight hundred and thirty-eight! Miraculous circumstance! extraordinary fulfilment of a prediction of the planets!

TOM. What are you talking about?

MR. STARGAZER (*looking about*). Is there nobody else in sight, up the street or down? No, not a soul! This, then, is the man whose coming was revealed to me by the stars, six months ago!

TOM. What do you mean?

MR. STARGAZER. Young man, that I have consulted the Book of Fate with rare and wonderful success,—that coming events have cast their shadows before.

TOM. Don't talk nonsense to me,—I ain't an event; I'm a lamplighter!

MR. STARGAZER (*aside*). True!—Strange destiny that one, announced by the planets as of noble birth, should be devoted to so humble an occupation. (*Aloud.*) But you were not *always* a lamplighter?

TOM. Why, no. I wasn't born with a ladder on my left shoulder, and a light in my other hand. But I took to it very early, though,—I had it from my uncle.

MR. STARGAZER (*aside*). He had it from his uncle! How plain, and yet how forcible, is his language! He speaks of lamplighting, as though it were the whooping-cough or measles! (*To him.*) Ay!

TOM. Yes, he was the original. You should have known him!— 'cod! he was a genius, if ever there was one. Gas was the death of him! When gas lamps was first talked of, my uncle draws himself up, and says, 'I'll not believe it, there's no sich a thing,' he says. 'You might as well talk of laying on an everlasting succession of glow-worms!' But when they made the experiment of lighting a piece of Pall Mall——

MR. STARGAZER. That was when it first came up?

TOM. No, no, that was when it was first laid down. Don't mind me; I can't help a joke, now and then. My uncle was sometimes took that way. When the experiment was made of lighting a piece of Pall Mall, and he had actually witnessed it, with his own eyes, you should have seen my uncle then!

MR. STARGAZER. So much overcome?

TOM. Overcome, sir! He fell off his ladder, from weakness, fourteen times that very night; and his last fall was into a wheelbarrow that was going his way, and humanely took him home. 'I foresee in this,' he says, 'the breaking up of our profession; no more polishing of the tin reflectors,' he says; 'no more fancy-work, in the way of clipping the cottons at two o'clock in the morning; no more going the rounds to trim by daylight, and dribbling down of the *ile* on the hats and bonnets of the ladies and gentlemen, when one feels in good spirits. Any low fellow can light a gas-lamp, and it's all up!' So he petitioned the Government for—what do you call that that they give to people when it's found out that they've never been of any use, and have been paid too much for doing nothing?

MR. STARGAZER. Compensation?

TOM. Yes, that's the thing,—compensation. They didn't give him any, though! And then he got very fond of his country all at once, and went about, saying how that the bringing in of gas was a death-blow to his native land, and how that its *ile* and cotton trade was gone for ever, and the whales would go and kill themselves, privately, in spite and vexation at not being caught! After this, he was right-down cracked, and called his 'bacco pipe a gas pipe, and thought his tears was lamp *ile*, and all manner of nonsense. At last, he went and hung himself on a lamp iron, in St. Martin's Lane, that he'd always been very fond of; and as he was a remarkably good husband, and had never had any secrets from his wife, he put a note in the two-penny post, as he went along, to tell the widder where the body was.

MR. STARGAZER (*laying his hand upon his arm, and speaking mysteriously*). Do you remember your parents?

TOM. My mother I do, very well!

MR. STARGAZER. Was she of noble birth?

TOM. Pretty well. She was in the mangling line. Her mother came of a highly respectable family,—such a business, in the sweet-stuff and hardbake way!

MR. STARGAZER. Perhaps your father was——

TOM. Why, I hardly know about him. The fact is, there was some little doubt, at the time, who *was* my father. Two or three young gentlemen were paid the pleasing compliment; but their incomes being limited, they were compelled delicately to decline it.

MR. STARGAZER. Then the prediction is not fulfilled merely in part, but entirely and completely. Listen, young man,—I am acquainted with all the celestial bodies——

TOM. Are you, though?—I hope they are quite well,—every body.

MR. STARGAZER. Don't interrupt me. I am versed in the great sciences of astronomy and astrology; in my house there I have every description of apparatus for observing the course and motion of the planets. I'm writing a work about them, which will consist of eighty-four volumes, imperial quarto; and an appendix, nearly twice as long. I read what's going to happen in the stars.

TOM. Read what's going to happen in the stars! Will anything particular happen in the stars in the course of next week, now?

MR. STARGAZER. You don't understand me. I read in the stars what's going to happen here. Six months ago I derived from this source the knowledge that, precisely as the clock struck five, on the afternoon of this very day, a stranger would present himself before my enraptured sight,—that stranger would be a man of illustrious and high descent,—that stranger would be the destined husband of my young and lovely niece, who is now beneath that roof (*points to his house*);—that stranger is yourself : I receive you with open arms!

TOM. Me! I, the man of illustrious and high—I, the husband of a young and lovely—Oh! it can't be, you know! the stars have made a mistake—the comet has put 'em out!

MR. STARGAZER. Impossible! The characters were as plain as pikestaves. The clock struck five; you were here; there was not a soul in sight; a mystery envelopes your birth; you are a man of noble aspect. Does not everything combine to prove the accuracy of my observations?

TOM. Upon my word, it looks like it! And now I come to think of it, I have very often felt as if I wasn't the small beer I was taken for. And yet I don't know,—you're quite sure about the noble aspect?

MR. STARGAZER. Positively certain.

TOM. Give me your hand.

MR. STARGAZER. And my heart, too! (*They shake hands heartily.*)

TOM. The young lady is tolerably good-looking, is she?

MR. STARGAZER. Beautiful! A graceful carriage, an exquisite shape, a sweet voice; a countenance beaming with animation and expression; the eye of a startled fawn.

TOM. I see; a sort of game eye. Does she happen to have any of the—this is quite between you and me, you know,—and I only ask from curiosity,—not because I care about it,—any of the ready?

MR. STARGAZER. Five thousand pounds! But what of that? what of that? A word in your ear. I'm in search of the philosopher's stone! I have very nearly found it—not quite. It turns everything to gold; that's its property.

TOM. What a lot of property it must have!

MR. STARGAZER. When I get it, we'll keep it in the family. Not a word to any one! What will money be to us? We shall never be able to spend it fast enough.

TOM. Well, you know, we can but try,—I'll do my best endeavours.

MR. STARGAZER. Thank you,—thank you! But I'll introduce you to your future bride at once:—this way, this way!

TOM. What, without going my rounds first?

MR. STARGAZER. Certainly. A man in whom the planets take especial interest, and who is about to have a share in the philosopher's stone, descend to lamplighting!

TOM. Perish the base idea! not by no means! I'll take in my tools though, to prevent any kind inquiries after me, at your door. (*As he shoulders the ladder the sound of violent rain is heard.*) Holloa!

MR. STARGAZER (*putting his hand on his head in amazement*). What's that?

TOM. It's coming down, rather.

MR. STARGAZER. Rain!

TOM. Ah! and a soaker, too!

MR. STARGAZER. It can't be!—it's impossible!—(*Taking a book from his pocket, and turning over the pages hurriedly.*) Look here,—here it is,—here's the weather almanack,—'Set fair,'—I knew it couldn't be! (*with great triumph*).

TOM (*turning up his collar as the rain increases*). Don't you think there's a dampness in the atmosphere?

MR. STARGAZER (*looking up*). It's singular,—it's *like* rain!

TOM. Uncommonly like.

MR. STARGAZER. It's a mistake in the elements, somehow. Here it is, 'set fair,'—and set fair it ought to be. 'Light clouds floating about.' Ah! you see, there are no light clouds;—the weather's all wrong.

TOM. Don't you think we had better get under cover?

MR. STARGAZER (*slowly retreating towards the house*). I don't acknowledge that it has any right to rain, mind! I protest against this. If Nature goes on in this way, I shall lose all respect for her,—it won't do, you know; it ought to have been two degrees colder, yesterday; and instead of that, it was warmer. This is not the way to treat scientific men. I protest against it!

[*Exeunt into house, both talking, TOM pushing STARGAZER on, and the latter continually turning back, to declaim against the weather.*]

SCENE II.—*A Room in* STARGAZER'S *house,* BETSY MARTIN, EMMA STARGAZER, FANNY BROWN, *and* GALILEO, *all murmuring together as they enter.*

BETSY. I say again, young ladies, that it's shameful! unbearable!

ALL. Oh! shameful! shameful!

BETSY. Marry Miss Emma to a great, old, ugly, doting, dreaming As-tron-o-Magician, like Mr. Mooney, who's always winking and blinking through telescopes and that, and can't see a pretty face when it's under his very nose!

GALILEO (*with a melancholy air*). There never was a pretty face under *his* nose, Betsy, leastways, since I've known him. He's very plain.

BETSY. Ah! there's poor young master, too; he hasn't even spirits enough left to laugh at his own jokes. I'm sure I pity him, from the very bottom of my heart.

FANNY *and* EMMA. Poor fellow!

GALILEO. Ain't I a legitimate subject for pity! Ain't it a dreadful thing that I, that am twenty-one come next Lady-day, should be treated like a little boy?—and all because my father is so busy with the moon's age that he don't care about mine; and so much occupied in making observations on the sun round which the earth revolves, that he takes no notice of the son that revolves round him! I wasn't taken out of nankeen frocks and trousers till I became quite unpleasant in 'em.

ALL. What a shame!

GALILEO. I wasn't, indeed. And look at me now! Here's a state of things. Is this a suit of clothes for a major,—at least, for a gentleman who is a minor now, but will be a major on the very next Lady-day that comes? Is this a fit——

ALL (*interrupting him*). Certainly not!

GALILEO (*vehemently*). I won't stand it—I won't submit to it any longer. I *will* be married.

ALL. No, no, no! don't be rash.

GALILEO. I will, I tell you. I'll marry my cousin Fanny. Give me a kiss, Fanny; and Emma and Betsy will look the other way the while. (*Kisses her.*) There!

BETSY. Sir—sir! here's your father coming!

GALILEO. Well, then, I'll have another, as an antidote to my father. One more; Fanny. (*Kisses her.*)

MR. STARGAZER (*without*). This way! this way! You shall behold her immediately.

Enter MR. STARGAZER, TOM *following bashfully.*

MR. STARGAZER. Where is my——? Oh, here she is! Fanny, my dear, come here. Do you see that gentleman? (*Aside.*)

FANNY. What gentleman, uncle? Do you mean that elastic person yonder who is bowing with so much perseverance?

MR. STARGAZER. Hush! yes; that's the interesting stranger.

FANNY. Why, he is kissing his hand, uncle. What does the creature mean?

MR. STARGAZER. Ah, the rogue! Just like me, before I married your poor aunt,—all fire and impatience. He means love, my darling, love. I've such a delightful surprise for you. I didn't tell you before, for fear there should be any mistake; but it's all right, it's all right. The stars have settled it all among 'em. He's to be your husband!

FANNY. My husband, uncle? Goodness gracious, Emma! (*Converses apart with her.*)

MR. STARGAZER (*aside*). He has made a sensation already. His noble aspect and distinguished air have produced an instantaneous impression. Mr. Grig, will you permit me? (TOM *advances awkwardly.*)—This is my niece, Mr. Grig,—my niece, Miss Fanny Brown; my daughter, Emma,—Mr. Thomas Grig, the favourite of the planets.

TOM. I hope I see Miss Hemmer in a conwivial state? (*Aside to* MR. STARGAZER.) I say, I don't know which is which.

MR. STARGAZER (*aside*). The young lady nearest here is your affianced bride. Say something appropriate.

TOM. Certainly; yes, of course. Let me see. Miss (*crosses to her*)—I—thank'ee! (*Kisses her, behind his hat. She screams.*)

GALILEO (*bursting from* BETSY, *who has been retaining him*). Outrageous insolence! (BETSY *runs off.*)

MR. STARGAZER. Halloa, sir, halloa!

TOM. Who is this juvenile salamander, sir?

MR. STARGAZER. My little boy,—only my little boy; don't mind him. Shake hands with the gentleman, sir, instantly (*to* GALILEO).

TOM. A very fine boy, indeed! and he does you great credit, sir. How d'ye do, my little man? (*They shake hands,* GALILEO *looking very wrathful, as* TOM *pats him on the head.*) There, that's very right and proper. ''Tis dogs delight to bark and bite'; not young gentlemen, you know. There, there!

MR. STARGAZER. Now let me introduce you to that *sanctum sanctorum,*—that hallowed ground,—that philosophical retreat—where I, the *genius loci,*——

TOM. Eh?

MR. STARGAZER. The *genius loci*——

TOM (*aside*). Something to drink, perhaps. Oh, ah! yes, yes!

MR. STARGAZER. Have made all my greatest and most profound discoveries! where the telescope has almost grown to my eye with constant application; and the glass retort has been shivered to pieces from the ardour with which my experiments have been pursued. There the illustrious Mooney is, even now, pursuing those researches which will enrich us with precious metal, and make us masters of the world. Come, Mr. Grig.

TOM. By all means, sir; and luck to the illustrious Mooney, say I, —not so much on Mooney's account as for our noble selves.

MR. STARGAZER. Emma!

EMMA. Yes, papa.

MR. STARGAZER. The same day that makes your cousin Mrs. Grig, will make you and that immortal man, of whom we have just now spoken, one.

EMMA. Oh! consider, dear papa,——

MR. STARGAZER. You are unworthy of him, I know; but he,— kind, generous creature,—consents to overlook your defects, and to take you, for my sake,—devoted man!—Come, Mr. Grig!—Galileo Isaac Newton Flamstead!

GALILEO. Well? (*Advancing sulkily.*)

MR. STARGAZER. In name, alas! but not in nature; knowing, even by sight, no other planets than the sun and moon,—here is your weekly pocket-money,—sixpence! Take it all!

TOM. And don't spend it all at once, my man! Now, sir!

MR. STARGAZER. Now, Mr. Grig,—go first, sir, I beg!

[*Exeunt* TOM *and* MR. STARGAZER.

GALILEO. 'Come, Mr. Grig!'—'Go first, Mr. Grig!'—'Day that makes your cousin Mrs. Grig!'—I'll secretly stick a penknife into Mr. Grig, if I live to be three hours older!

FANNY (*on one side of him*). Oh! don't talk in that desperate way, —there's a dear, dear creature!

EMMA (*on the other side*). No! pray do not;—it makes my blood run cold to hear you.

GALILEO. Oh! if I was of age!—if I was only of age!—or we could go to Gretna Green, at threepence a head, including refreshments and all incidental expenses. But that could never be! Oh! if I was only of age!

FANNY. But what if you were? What could you do, then?

GALILEO. Marry you, cousin Fanny; I could marry you then lawfully, and without anybody's consent.

FANNY. You forget that, situated as we are, we could not be

married, even if you *were* one-and-twenty;—we have no money!

EMMA. Not even enough for the fees!

GALILEO. Oh! I am sure every Christian clergyman, under such afflicting circumstances, would marry us on credit. The wedding-fees might stand over till the first christening, and then we could settle the little bill altogether. Oh! why ain't I of age!—why ain't I of age?

Enter BETSY, *in haste.*

BETSY. Well! I never could have believed it! There, Miss! I wouldn't have believed it, if I had dreamt it, even with a bit of bride-cake under my pillow! To dare to go and think of marrying a young lady, with five thousand pounds, to a common lamplighter!

ALL. A lamplighter?

BETSY. Yes, he's Tom Grig the lamplighter, and nothing more nor less, and old Mr. Stargazer goes and picks him out of the open street, and brings him in for Miss Fanny's husband, because he pretends to have read something about it in the stars. Stuff and nonsense! I don't believe he knows his letters in the stars, and that's the truth; or if he's got as far as words in one syllable, it's quite as much as he has.

FANNY. Was such an atrocity ever heard of? I, left with no power to marry without his consent, and he almost possessing the power to force my inclinations.

EMMA. It's actually worse than my being sacrificed to that odious and detestable Mr. Mooney.

BETSY. Come, Miss, it's not quite so bad as that neither; for Thomas Grig is a young man, and a proper young man enough too, but as to Mr. Mooney,—oh, dear! no husband is bad enough in my opinion, Miss; but he is worse than nothing, —a great deal worse.

FANNY. You seem to speak feelingly about this same Mr. Grig.

BETSY. Oh, dear no, Miss, not I. I don't mean to say but what Mr. Grig may be very well in his way, Miss; but Mr. Grig and I have never held any communication together, not even so much as how-d'ye-do. Oh, no indeed, I have been very careful, Miss, as I always am with strangers. I was acquainted with the last lamplighter, Miss, but he's going to be married, and has given up the calling, for the young woman's parents being very respectable, wished her to marry a literary man, and so he has set up as a bill-sticker. Mr. Grig only came upon this beat at five to-night, Miss.

FANNY. Which is a very sufficient reason why you don't know more of him.

BETSY. Well, Miss, perhaps it is; and I hope there's no crime in making friends in this world, if we can, Miss.

FANNY. Certainly not. So far from it, that I most heartily wish you could make something more than a friend of this Mr. Grig, and so lead him to falsify this prediction.

GALILEO. Oh! don't you think you could, Betsy?

EMMA. You could not manage at the same time to get any young friend of yours to make something more than a friend of Mr. Mooney, could you, Betsy?

GALILEO. But, seriously, don't you think you could manage to give us all a helping hand together, in some way, eh, Betsy?

FANNY. Yes, yes, that would be so delightful. I should be grateful to her for ever. Shouldn't you?

EMMA. Oh, to the very end of my life!

GALILEO. And so should I, you know, and lor'! we should make her so rich, when—when we got rich ourselves,—shouldn't we?

BOTH. Oh, that we should, of course.

BETSY. Let me see. I don't wish to have Mr. Grig to myself, you know. I don't want to be married.

ALL. No! no! no! Of course she don't.

BETSY. I haven't the least idea to put Mr. Grig off this match, you know, for anybody's sake, but you young people's. I am going quite *contrairy* to my own feelings, you know.

ALL. Oh, yes, yes! How kind she is!

BETSY. Well, I'll go over the matter with the young ladies in Miss Emma's room, and if we can think of anything that seems likely to help us, so much the better; and if we can't, we're none the worst. But Master Galileo mustn't come, for he is so horrid jealous of Miss Fanny that I dursn't hardly say anything before him. Why, I declare (*looking off*), there is my gentleman looking about him as if he had lost Mr. Stargazer, and now he turns this way. There.—get out of sight. Make haste!

GALILEO. I may see 'em as far as the bottom stair, mayn't I, Betsy?

BETSY. Yes, but not a step farther on any consideration. There, get away softly, so that if he passes here, he may find me alone. (*They creep gently out*, GALILEO *returns and peeps in*.)

GALILEO. Hist, Betsy!

BETSY. Go away, sir. What have you come back for?

GALILEO (*holding out a large pin*). I wish you'd take an opportunity of sticking this a little way into him for patting me on the head just now.

BETSY. Nonsense, you can't afford to indulge in such expensive amusements as retaliation yet awhile. You must wait till you come into your property, sir. There—Get you gone!

[*Exit* GALILEO.

Enter TOM GRIG.

TOM (*aside*). I never saw such a scientific file in my days. The enterprising gentleman that drowned himself *to see how it felt*, is nothing to him. There he is, just gone down to the bottom of a dry well in an uncommonly small bucket, to take an extra squint at the stars, they being seen best, I suppose, through the medium of a cold in the head. Halloa! Here is a young female of attractive proportions. I wonder now whether a man of noble aspect would be justified in tickling her. (*He advances stealthily and tickles her under the arm*.)

BETSY (*starting*). Eh! what! Lor', sir!

TOM. Don't be alarmed. My intentions are strictly honourable. In other words, I have no intentions whatever.

BETSY. Then you ought to be more careful, Mr. Grig. That was a liberty, sir.

TOM. I know it was. The cause of liberty, all over the world,— that's my sentiment! What is your name?

BETSY (*curtseying*). Betsy Martin, sir.

TOM. A name famous both in song and story. Would you have the goodness, Miss Martin, to direct me to that particular apartment wherein the illustrious Mooney is now pursuing his researches?

BETSY (*aside*). A little wholesome fear may not be amiss. (*To him, in assumed agitation*.) You are not going into *that* room, Mr. Grig?

TOM. Indeed, I am, and I ought to be there now, having promised to join that light of science, your master (a short six by the bye!), outside the door.

BETSY. That dreadful and mysterious chamber! Another victim!

TOM. Victim, Miss Martin!

BETSY. Oh! the awful oath of secrecy which binds me not to disclose the perils of that gloomy, hideous room.

TOM (*astonished*). Miss Martin!

BETSY. Such a fine young man,—so rosy and fresh-coloured, that he should fall into the clutches of that cruel and insatiable monster! I cannot continue to witness such frightful scenes; I must give warning.

TOM. If you have anything to unfold, young woman, have the goodness to give *me* warning at once.

BETSY (*affecting to recover herself*). No, no, Mr. Grig, it's nothing,—it's ha! ha! ha!—don't mind me, don't mind me, but it certainly is very shocking;—no,—no,—I don't mean that. I mean funny,—yes. Ha! ha! ha!

TOM (*aside, regarding her attentively*). I suspect a trick here,— some other lover in the case who wants to come over the stars; —but it won't do. I'll tell you what, young woman (*to her*), if this is a cloak, you had better try it on elsewhere;—in plain English, if you have any object to gain and think to gain it by frightening *me*, it's all my eye and, and—yourself, Miss Martin.

BETSY. Well, then, if you will rush upon your fate,—there (*pointing off*)—that's the door at the end of that long passage and across the gravelled yard. The room is built away from the house on purpose.

TOM. I'll make for it at once, and the first object I inspect through that same telescope, which now and then grows to your master's eye, shall be the moon—the moon, which is the emblem of your inconstant and deceitful sex, Miss Martin.

Duet.

AIR—'*The Young May-moon.*'

TOM.   There comes a new moon twelve times a year.

BETSY.   And when there is none, all is dark and drear.

TOM.   In which I espy—

BETSY.   And so, too, do I—

BOTH.   A resemblance to womankind very clear.

BOTH. There comes a new moon twelve times in a year;
And when there is none, all is dark and drear.
TOM. In which I espy—
BETSY. And so do I—
BOTH. A resemblance to womankind very clear.

Second Verse.

TOM. She changes, she's fickle, she drives men mad.
BETSY. She comes to bring light, and leaves them sad.
TOM. So restless wild—
BETSY. But so sweetly wild—
BOTH. That no better companion could be had.
BOTH. There comes a new moon twelve times a year;
And when there is none, all is dark and drear.
TOM. In which I espy—
BETSY. And so do I—
BOTH. A resemblance to womankind very clear. [*Exeunt.*

SCENE III.—*A large gloomy room; a window with a telescope directed towards the sky without, a table covered with books, instruments and apparatus, which are also scattered about in other parts of the chamber, a dim lamp, a pair of globes, etc., a skeleton in a case, and various uncouth objects displayed against the walls. Two doors in flat. MR. MOONEY discovered, with a very dirty face, busily engaged in blowing a fire, upon which is a crucible.*

Enter MR. STARGAZER, with a lamp, beckoning to TOM GRIG, who enters with some unwillingness.

MR. STARGAZER. This, Mr. Grig, is the *sanctum sanctorum* of which I have already spoken; this is at once the laboratory and observatory.
TOM. It's not an over-lively place, is it?
MR. STARGAZER. It has an air of solemnity which well accords with the great and mysterious pursuits that are here in constant prosecution, Mr. Grig.
TOM. Ah! I should think it would suit an undertaker to the life; or perhaps I should rather say to the death. What may that cheerful object be now? (*Pointing to a large phial.*)

MR. STARGAZER. That contains a male infant with three heads, —we use it in astrology;—it is supposed to be a *charm*.

TOM. I shouldn't have supposed it myself, from his appearance. The young gentleman isn't alive, is he?

MR. STARGAZER. No, he is preserved in spirits. (MR. MOONEY *sneezes*.)

TOM (*retreating into a corner*). Halloa! What the—— (MR. MOONEY *looks vacantly round*.) That gentleman, I suppose, is out of spirits?

MR. STARGAZER (*laying his hand upon* TOM'S *arm and looking toward the philosopher*). Hush! that is the gifted Mooney. Mark well his noble countenance,—intense thought beams from every lineament. That is the great astrologer.

TOM. He looks as if he had been having a touch at the black art. I say, why don't he say something?

MR. STARGAZER. He is in a state of abstraction; see he directs his bellows this way, and blows upon the empty air.

TOM. Perhaps he sees a strange spark in this direction and wonders how he came here. I wish he'd blow me out. (*Aside*.) I don't half like this.

MR. STARGAZER. You shall see me rouse him.

TOM. Don't put yourself out of the way on my account; I can make his acquaintance at any other time.

MR. STARGAZER. No time like the time present. Nothing awakens him from these fits of meditation but an electric shock. We always have a strongly charged battery on purpose. I'll give him a shock directly. (MR. STARGAZER *goes up and cautiously places the end of a wire in* MR. MOONEY'S *hand. He then stoops down beside the table as though bringing it in contact with the battery.* MR. MOONEY *immediately jumps up with a loud cry and throws away the bellows*.)

TOM (*squaring at the philosopher*). It wasn't me, you know,— none of your nonsense.

MR. STARGAZER (*comes hastily forward*). Mr. Grig,—Mr. Grig, —not that disrespectful attitude to one of the greatest men that ever lived. This, my dear friend (*to* MOONEY),—is the noble stranger.

MR. MOONEY. A ha!

MR. STARGAZER. Who arrived, punctual to his time, this afternoon.

MR. MOONEY. O ho!

MR. STARGAZER. Welcome him, my friend,—give him your hand. (MR. MOONEY *appears confused and raises his leg.*) No—no, that's your foot. So absent, Mr. Grig, in his gigantic meditations that very often he doesn't know one from the other. Yes, that's your hand, very good, my dear friend, very good (*pats* MOONEY *on the back, as he and* TOM *shake hands, the latter at arm's length*).

MR. STARGAZER. Have you made any more discoveries during my absence?

MR. MOONEY. Nothing particular.

MR. STARGAZER. Do you think—do you think, my dear friend, that we shall arrive at any great stage in our labours, anything at all approaching to their final consummation in the course of the night?

MR. MOONEY. I cannot take upon myself to say.

MR. STARGAZER. What are your opinions upon the subject?

MR. MOONEY. I haven't any opinions upon any subject whatsoever.

MR. STARGAZER. Wonderful man! Here's a mind, Mr. Grig.

TOM. Yes, his conversation's very improving indeed. But what's he staring so hard at me for?

MR. STARGAZER. Something occurs to him. Don't speak,—don't disturb the current of his reflections upon any account. (MR. MOONEY *walks solemnly up to* TOM, *who retreats before him; taking off his hat turns it over and over with a thoughtful countenance and finally puts it upon his own head.*)

MR. STARGAZER. Eccentric man!

TOM. I say, I hope he don't mean to keep that, because if he does, his eccentricity is unpleasant. Give him another shock and knock it off, will you?

MR. STARGAZER. Hush! hush! not a word. (MR. MOONEY, *keeping his eyes fixed on* TOM, *slowly returns to* MR. STARGAZER *and whispers in his ear.*)

MR. STARGAZER. Surely; by all means. I took the date of his birth, and all other information necessary for the purpose just now. (*To* TOM.) Mr. Mooney suggests that we should cast your nativity without delay, in order that we may communicate to you your future destiny.

MR. MOONEY. Let us retire for that purpose.

MR. STARGAZER. Certainly, wait here for a few moments, Mr. Grig : we are only going into the little laboratory and will return immediately. Now, my illustrious friend. (*He takes up a lamp and leads the way to one of the doors. As* MR. MOONEY *follows,* TOM *steals behind him and regains his hat.* MR. MOONEY *turns round, stares, and exit through door.*)

TOM. Well, that's the queerest genius I ever came across,—rather a singular person for a little smoking party. (*Looks into the crucible.*) This is the saucepan, I suppose, where they're boiling the philosopher's stone down to the proper consistency. I hope it's nearly done; when it's quite ready, I'll send out for six-penn'orth of sprats, and turn 'em into gold fish for a first experiment. 'Cod! it'll be a comfortable thing though to have no end to one's riches. I'll have a country house and a park, and I'll plant a bit of it with a double row of gas-lamps a mile long, and go out with a French polished mahogany ladder, and two servants in livery behind me, to light 'em with my own hands every night. What's to be seen here? (*Looks through telescope.*) Nothing particular, the stopper being on at the other end. The little boy with three heads (*looking towards the case*). What a comfort he must have been to his parents!—Halloa! (*taking up a large knife*) this is a disagreeable-looking instrument,—something too large for bread and cheese, or oysters, and not of a bad shape for sticking live persons in the ribs. A very dismal place this,—I wish they'd come back. Ah!— (*coming upon the skeleton*) here's a ghastly object,—what does the writing say?—(*reads a label upon the case*) 'Skeleton of a gentleman prepared by Mr. Mooney.' I hope Mr. Mooney may not be in the habit of inviting gentlemen here, and making 'em into such preparations without their own consent. Here's a book, now. What's all this about, I wonder? The letters look as if a steam-engine had printed 'em by accident. (*Turns over the leaves, spelling to himself.*)

GALILEO *enters softly unseen by* TOM, *who has his back towards him.*

GALILEO (*aside*). Oh, you're there, are you? If I could but suffocate him, not for life, but only till I am one-and-twenty, and then revive him, what a comfort and convenience it would be!

I overheard my cousin Fanny talking to Betsy about coming here. What can she want here? If she can be false,—false to *me*;—it seems impossible, but if she is?—well, well, we shall see. If I can reach that lumber-room unseen, Fanny Brown,—beware. (*He steals toward the door on the* L.—*opens it, and exit cautiously into the room. As he does so,* TOM *turns the other way.*)

TOM (*closing the book*). It's very pretty Greek, I think. What a time they are!

MR. STARGAZER *and* MOONEY *enter from room.*

MOONEY. Tell the noble gentleman of his irrevocable destiny.

MR. STARGAZER (*with emotion*). No,—no, prepare him first.

TOM (*aside*). Prepare him! 'prepared by Mr. Mooney.'—This is a case of kidnapping and slaughter. (*To them.*) Let him attempt to prepare me at his peril!

MR. STARGAZER. Mr. Grig, why this demonstration?

TOM. Oh, don't talk to me of demonstration;—you ain't going to demonstrate me, and so I tell you.

MR. STARGAZER. Alas! (*Crossing to him.*) The truth we have to communicate requires but little demonstration from our feeble lips. We have calculated upon your nativity.

MOONEY. Yes, we have, we have.

MR. STARGAZER. Tender-hearted man! (MOONEY *weeps.*) See there, Mr. Grig, isn't that affecting?

TOM. What is he piping his boiled gooseberry eye for, sir? How should I know whether it's affecting or not?

MR. STARGAZER. For you, for you. We find that you will expire to-morrow two months, at thirty minutes—wasn't it thirty minutes, my friend?

MOONEY. Thirty-five minutes, twenty-seven seconds, and five-sixths of a second. Oh! (*Groans.*)

MR. STARGAZER. Thirty-five minutes, twenty-seven seconds, and five-sixths of a second past nine o'clock.

MOONEY. A.M. (*They both wipe their eyes.*)

TOM (*alarmed*). Don't tell me, you've made a mistake somewhere; —I won't believe it.

MOONEY. No, it's all correct, we worked it all in the most satisfactory manner.—Oh! (*Groans again.*)

Tom. Satisfactory, sir! Your notions of the satisfactory are of an extraordinary nature.

Mr. Stargazer (*producing a pamphlet*). It is confirmed by the prophetic almanack. Here is the prediction for to-morrow two months,—'The decease of a great person may be looked for about this time.'

Tom (*dropping into his chair*). That's me! It's all up! inter me decently, my friends.

Mr. Stargazer (*shaking his hand*). Your wishes shall be attended to. We must have the marriage with my niece at once, in order that your distinguished race may be transmitted to posterity. Condole with him, my Mooney, while I compose my feelings, and settle the preliminaries of the marriage in solitude.

> (*Takes up lamp and exit into room* R. Mooney *draws up a chair in a line with* Tom, *a long way off. They both sigh heavily.* Galileo *opens the lumber-room door. As he does so the room door opens and* Betsy *steals softly in, beckoning to* Emma *and* Fanny *who follow. He retires again abruptly.*)

Betsy (*aside.*) Now, young ladies, if you take heart only for one minute you may frighten Mr. Mooney out of being married at once.

Emma. But if he has serious thoughts?

Betsy. Nonsense, Miss, he hasn't any thoughts. Your papa says to him, 'Will you marry my daughter?' and he says, 'Yes, I will'; and he would and will if you ain't bold, but bless you, he never turned it over in his mind for a minute. If you, Miss (*to* Emma), pretend to hate him and love a rival, and you, Miss (*to* Fanny), to love him to distraction, you'll frighten him so betwixt you that he'll declare off directly, I warrant. The love will frighten him quite as much as the hate. He never saw a woman in a passion, and as to one in love, I don't believe that anybody but his mother ever kissed that grumpy old face of his in all his born days. Now, do try him, ladies. Come, we're losing time.

> (*She conceals herself behind the skeleton case.* Emma *rushes up to* Tom Grig *and embraces him, while* Fanny *clasps* Mooney *round the neck.* Galileo *appears at his door in an attitude of amazement, and* Mr. Stargazer *at his, after running in again with the lamp, which before he sees*

what is going forward he had in his hand. TOM *and*
MOONEY *in great astonishment.*)

FANNY (*to* MOONEY). ⎱
EMMA (*to* GRIG).   ⎰ Hush! hush!

(TOM GRIG *and* MOONEY *get their heads sufficiently out of the
embrace to exchange a look of wonder.*)

EMMA. Dear Mr. Grig, I know you must consider this strange,
extraordinary, unaccountable conduct.

TOM. Why, ma'am, without explanation, it does appear singular.

EMMA. Yes, yes, I know it does, I know it will, but the urgency
of the case must plead my excuse. Too fascinating Mr. Grig,
I have seen you once and only once, but the impression of that
maddening interview can never be effaced. I love you to distraction. (*Falls upon his shoulder.*)

TOM. You're extremely obliging ma'am, it's a flattering sort of
thing,—or it would be (*aside*) if I was going to live a little
longer,—but you're not the one, ma'am;—it's the other lady
that the stars have——

FANNY (*to* MOONEY). Nay, wonderful being, hear me—this is not
a time for false conventional delicacy. Wrapt in your sublime
visions, you have not perceived the silent tokens of a woman's
first and all-absorbing attachment, which have been, I fear,
but too perceptible in the eyes of others; but now I must speak
out. I hate this odious man. You are my first and only love.
Oh! speak to me.

MOONEY. I haven't anything appropriate to say, young woman.
I think I had better go. (*Attempting to get away.*)

FANNY. Oh! no, no, no (*detaining him*). Give me some encouragement. Not one kind word? not one look of love?

MOONEY. I don't know how to look a look of love.—I'm, I'm
frightened.

TOM. So am I! I don't understand this. I tell you, Miss, that the
other lady is my destined wife. Upon my word you mustn't
hug me, you'll make her jealous.

FANNY. Jealous! of you! Hear me (*to* MOONEY). I renounce all
claim or title to the hand of that or any other man and vow to
be eternally and wholly yours.

MOONEY. No, don't, you can't be mine,—nobody can be mine.—
I don't want anybody—I—I——

EMMA. If you will not hear her—hear *me*, detested monster.—

84

Hear me declare that sooner than be your bride, with this deep passion for another rooted in my heart,—I——

MOONEY. You need not make any declaration on the subject, young woman.

MR. STARGAZER (*coming forward*). She shan't,—she shan't. That's right, don't hear her. She shall marry you whether she likes it or not,—she shall marry you to-morrow morning,—and you, Miss (*to* FANNY), shall marry Mr. Grig if I trundle you to church in a wheelbarrow.

GALILEO (*coming forward*). So she shall! so she may! Let her! let her! I give her leave.

MR. STARGAZER. You give her leave, you young dog! Who the devil cares whether *you* give her leave or not? and what are you spinning about in that way for?

GALILEO. I'm fierce, I'm furious,—don't talk to me,—I shall do somebody a mischief;—I'll never marry anybody after this, never, never, it isn't safe. I'll live and die a bachelor!—there— a bachelor! a bachelor! (*He goes up and encounters* BETSY. *She talks to him apart, and his wrath seems gradually to subside.*)

MOONEY. The little boy, albeit of tender years, has spoken wisdom. I have been led to the contemplation of womankind. I find their love is too violent for my staid habits. I would rather not venture upon the troubled waters of matrimony.

MR. STARGAZER. You don't mean to marry my daughter? Not if I say she *shall* have you? (MOONEY *shakes his head solemnly*.) Mr. Grig, you have not changed your mind because of a little girlish folly?

TOM. To-morrow two months! I may as well get through as much gold as I can in the meantime. Why, sir, if the pot nearly boils (*pointing to the crucible*),—if you're pretty near the philosopher's stone,——

MR. STARGAZER. Pretty near! We're sure of it—certain; it's as good as money in the Bank. (GALILEO *and* BETSY, *who have been listening attentively, bustle about, fanning the fire, and throwing in sundry powders from the bottles on the table, then cautiously retire to a distance.*)

TOM. If that's the case, sir, I am ready to keep faith with the planets. I'll take her, sir, I'll take her.

MR. STARGAZER. Then here's her hand, Mr. Grig,—no resistance,

Miss (*drawing* FANNY *forward*). It's of no use, so you may as well do it with a good grace. Take her hand, Mr. Grig. (*The crucible blows up with a loud crash; they all start.*)

MR. STARGAZER. What!—the labour of fifteen years destroyed in an instant!

MOONEY (*stooping over the fragments*). That's the only disappointment I have experienced in this process since I was first engaged in it when I was a boy. It always blows up when it's on the point of succeeding.

TOM. Is the philosopher stone gone?

MOONEY. No.

TOM. Not gone, sir?

MOONEY. No—it never came!

MR. STARGAZER. But we'll get it, Mr. Grig. Don't be cast down, we shall discover it in less than fifteen years this time, I dare say.

TOM (*relinquishing* FANNY'S *hand.*) Ah! Were the stars very positive about this union?

MR. STARGAZER. They had not a doubt about it. They said it *was* to be, and it must be. They were peremptory.

TOM. I am sorry for that, because they have been very civil to me in the way of showing a light now and then, and I really regret disappointing 'em. But under the peculiar circumstances of the case, it can't be.

MR. STARGAZER. Can't be, Mr. Grig! What can't be?

TOM. The marriage, sir. I forbid the banns. (*Retires and sits down.*)

MR. STARGAZER. Impossible! such a prediction unfulfilled! Why, the consequences would be as fatal as those of a concussion between the comet and this globe. Can't be! it must be, shall be.

BETSY (*coming forward, followed by* GALILEO). If you please, sir, may I say a word?

MR. STARGAZER. What have you got to say?—speak, woman!

BETSY. Why, sir, I don't think Mr. Grig is the right man.

MR. STARGAZER. What!

BETSY. Don't you recollect, sir, that just as the house-clock struck the first stroke of five, you gave Mr. Galileo a thump on the head with the butt end of your telescope, and told him to get out of the way?

MR. STARGAZER. Well, if I did, what of that?

BETSY. Why, then, sir, I say, and I would say it if I was to be killed for it, that he's the young gentleman that ought to marry Miss Fanny, and that the stars never meant anything else.

MR. STARGAZER. He! Why, he's a little boy.

GALILEO. I ain't. I'm one-and-twenty next Lady-day.

MR. STARGAZER. Eh! Eighteen hundred and—why, so he is, I declare. He's quite a stranger to me, certainly. I never thought about his age since he was fourteen, and I remember that birthday, because he'd a new suit of clothes then. But the noble family——

BETSY. Lor', sir! ain't it being of noble family to be the son of such a clever man as you?

MR. STARGAZER. That's true. And my mother's father would have been Lord Mayor, only he died of turtle the year before.

BETSY. Oh, it's quite clear.

MR. STARGAZER. The only question is about the time, because the church struck afterwards. But I should think the stars, taking so much interest in my house, would most likely go by the house-clock,—eh! Mooney?

MOONEY. Decidedly,—yes.

MR. STARGAZER. Then you may have her, my son. Her father was a great astronomer; so I hope that, though you *are* a blockhead, your children may be scientific. There! (*Joins their hands.*)

EMMA. Am I free to marry who I like, papa?

MR. STARGAZER. Won't you, Mooney? Won't you?

MOONEY. If anybody asks me to again I'll run away, and never come back any more.

MR. STARGAZER. Then we must drop the subject. Yes, your choice is now unfettered.

EMMA. Thank you, dear papa. Then I'll look about for somebody who will suit me without the delay of an instant longer than is absolutely necessary.

MR. STARGAZER. How very dutiful!

FANNY. And, as my being here just now with Emma was a little trick of Betsy's, I hope you'll forgive her, uncle.

EMMA.
GALILEO. } Oh, yes, do.

FANNY. And even reward her, uncle, for being instrumental in fulfilling the prediction.

EMMA. ⎫
GALILEO. ⎭ Oh, yes; do reward her—do.

FANNY. Perhaps you could find a husband for her, uncle, you know. Don't you understand?

BETSY. Pray don't mention it, Miss. I told you at first, Miss, that I had not the least wish or inclination to have Mr. Grig to myself. I couldn't abear that Mr. Grig should think I wanted him to marry me; oh no, Miss, not on any account.

MR. STARGAZER. Oh, that's pretty intelligible. Here, Mr. Grig. (*They fall back from his chair.*) Have you any objection to take this young woman for better, for worse?

BETSY. Lor', sir! how ondelicate!

MR. STARGAZER. I'll add a portion of ten pounds for your loss of time here to-night. What do you say, Mr. Grig?

TOM. It don't much matter. I ain't long for this world. Eight weeks of marriage might reconcile me to my fate. I should go off, I think, more resigned and peaceful. Yes, I'll take her, as a reparation. Come to my arms! (*He embraces her with a dismal face.*)

MR. STARGAZER (*taking a paper from his pocket*). Egad! that reminds me of what I came back to say, which all this bustle drove out of my head. There's a figure wrong in the nativity (*handing the paper to* MOONEY). He'll live to a green old age.

TOM (*looking up*). Eh! What?

MOONEY. So he will. Eighty-two years and twelve days will be the lowest.

TOM (*disengaging himself*). Eh! here! (*calling off*). Hallo, you, sir! bring in that ladder and lantern.

A Servant enters in great haste, and hands them to TOM.

SERVANT. There's such a row in the street,—none of the gas-lamps lit, and all the people calling for the lamplighter. *Such* a row! (*Rubbing his hands with great glee.*)

TOM. Is there, my fine fellow? Then I'll go and light 'em. And as, under existing circumstances, and with the prospect of a green old age before me, I'd rather *not* be married, Miss Martin, I beg to assure the ratepayers present that in future I shall pay the strictest attention to my professional duties, and do my best for the contractor; and that I shall be found upon my beat as long as they condescend to patronise the Lamplighter. (*Runs off*. MISS MARTIN *faints in the arms of* MOONEY.)

CURTAIN

MR. NIGHTINGALE'S DIARY

A Farce

IN ONE ACT
[1851]

BY CHARLES DICKENS AND
MARK LEMON

'Might I ask you,' said Nicholas, hesitating between the respect he ought to assume, and his love of the whimsical, 'might I ask you what the unities are?'

Mr. Curdle coughed and considered. 'The unities, sir,' he said, 'are a completeness—a kind of universal dovetailness with regard to place and time—a sort of general oneness, if I may be allowed to use so strong an expression. I take those to be the dramatic unities so far as I have been enabled to bestow attention upon them, and I have read much upon the subject, and thought much. I find, running through the performances of this child,' said Mr. Curdle, turning to the phenomenon, 'a unity of feeling, a breadth, a light and shade, a warmth of colouring, a tone, a harmony, a glow, an artistical development of original conceptions, which I look for, in vain, among older performers. I don't know whether I make myself understood?'

'Perfectly,' replied Nicholas.

'Just so,' said Mr. Curdle, pulling up his neckcloth. 'That is my definition of the unities of the drama.'

DRAMATIS PERSONÆ

At Devonshire House, Tuesday, *May* 27, 1851

Mr. Nightingale	Mr. Dudley Costello.
Mr. Gabblewig (*of the Middle Temple*)	Mr. Charles Dickens.
Tip (*his Tiger*)	Mr. Augustus Egg.
Slap (*professionally Mr. Formiville*)	Mr. Mark Lemon.
Lithers (*landlord of the 'Water-Lily'*)	Mr. Wilkie Collins.
Rosina	Miss Ellen Chaplin.
Susan	Mrs. Coe.

MR. NIGHTINGALE'S DIARY

SCENE.—*The Common Room of the Water-Lily Hotel at Malvern. Door and Window in flat. A carriage stops. Door-bell rings violently.*

TIP (*without*). Now, then! Wai-ter! Landlord! Somebody! (*Enter* TIP, *through door, with a quantity of luggage.*)

Enter LITHERS, L., *running in.*

LITHERS. Here you are, my boy.

TIP (*much offended*). My boy! Who are you boying of! Don't do it. I won't have it. The worm will turn if it's trod upon.

LITHERS. I never trod upon you.

TIP. What do you mean by calling *me* a worm?

LITHERS. You called yourself one. You ought to know what you are better than I do.

GABBLEWIG (*without*). Has anybody seen that puppy of mine—answers to the name of 'Tip'—with a gold-lace collar? (*Enters.*) O, here you are! You scoundrel, where have you been?

LITHERS. Good gracious me! Why, if it ain't Mr. Gabblewig, Junior!

GABBLEWIG. What, Lithers! Do *you* turn up at Malvern Wells, of all the places upon earth?

LITHERS. Bless you, sir, I've been landlord of this little place these two years! Ever since you did me that great kindness—ever since you paid out that execution for me when I was in the greengrocery way, and used to wait at your parties in the Temple—which is five years ago come Christmas—I've been (through a little legacy my wife dropped into) in the public line. I'm overjoyed to see you, sir. How do you do, sir? Do you find yourself pretty well, sir?

GABBLEWIG (*moodily seating himself*). Why, no, I can't say I *am* pretty well.

TIP. No more ain't I.

GABBLEWIG. Be so good as to take those boots of yours into the kitchen, sir.

TIP (*reluctantly*). Yes, sir.

GABBLEWIG. And the baggage into my bedroom.

TIP. Yes, sir. (*Aside.*) Here's a world!   [*Exit*, L.

LITHERS. The Queen's Counsellor, that is to be, looks very down —uncommonly down. Something's wrong. I wonder what it is. Can't be debt. Don't look like drinking. Hope it isn't dice! Ahem! Beg your pardon, Mr. Gabblewig, but you'd wish to dine, sir. He don't hear. (*Gets round, dusting the table as he goes, and at last stoops his head so as to come face to face with him.*) What would you choose for dinner, Mr. Gabblewig?

GABBLEWIG. O, ah, yes! Give me some cold veal.

LITHERS. Cold veal! He's out of his mind.

GABBLEWIG. I'm a miserable wretch. I *was* going to be married. I am *not* going to be married. The young lady's uncle refuses to consent. It's all off—all over—all up!

LITHERS. But there are other young ladies——

GABBLEWIG. Don't talk nonsense.

LITHERS (*aside*). All the rest are cold veal, I suppose. But,—you'll excuse my taking the liberty, being so much beholden to you, —but couldn't anything be done to get over the difficulty?

GABBLEWIG. Nothing at all. How's it possible? Do you know the nature of the uncle's objection? But of course you don't. I'll tell you. He says I speak too fast, and *am* too slow,—want reality of purpose, and all that. He says I'm all words. What the devil else does he suppose I *can* be, being a lawyer! He says I happen to be counsel for his daughter just now, but after marriage might be counsel for the opposite side. He says I am wanting in earnestness,—deficient in moral go-aheadism.

LITHERS. In which?

GABBLEWIG. Just so. In consequence of which you behold before you a crushed flower. I am shut up and done for,—the peace of the valley is fled;—I have come down here to see if the cold-water cure will have any effect on a broken heart. Having had a course of wet blanket, I am going to try the wet sheet; —dare say I shall finish before long with a daisy counterpane.

LITHERS (*aside*). Everybody's bit by the cold water. It will be the ruin of our business.

GABBLEWIG. If the waters of Malvern were the waters of Lethe,

I'd take a douche forty feet high, this afternoon, and drink
five-and-twenty tumblers before breakfast to-morrow morning.
Anything to wash out the tormenting remembrance of Rosina
Nightingale.

LITHERS. Nightingale, Mr. Gabblewig?

GABBLEWIG. Nightingale. As the Shakespeare duet went, in the
happy days of our amateur plays :

> The Nightingale alone,
> She, poor bird, as all forlorn,
> Lean'd her breast uptil a thorn.

I've no doubt she's doing it at the present moment—or leaning
her head against the drawing-room window, looking across the
Crescent. It's all the same.

LITHERS. The Crescent, Mr. Gabblewig?

GABBLEWIG. The Crescent.

LITHERS. Not at Bath?

GABBLEWIG. At Bath.

LITHERS (*feeling in his pockets*). Good gracious! (*Gives a letter.*)
Look at that, sir.

GABBLEWIG. The cramped hand of the obstinate old bird, who
might, could, and should have been—and wouldn't be my
father-in-law! (*Reads.*) 'Christopher Nightingale's compliments
to the landlord of the Water-Lily, at Malvern Wells.'

LITHERS. The present establishment.

GABBLEWIG (*reading*). 'And hearing it is a quiet, unpretending,
well-conducted house, requests to have the following rooms
prepared for him on Tuesday afternoon.'

LITHERS. The present afternoon.

GABBLEWIG (*reading*). 'Namely, a private sitting-room with a'—
what! a weed? He don't smoke.

LITHERS (*looking over his shoulder*). A view, sir.

GABBLEWIG. Oh! 'with a view.' Ay, ay. 'A bedroom for
Christopher N. with a'—what? with a wormy pew?

LITHERS (*looking over his shoulder*). A warming-pan.

GABBLEWIG. To be sure; but it's as like one as the other. 'With
a warming-pan, and two suitable chambers for Miss Rosina
Nightingale.'—Support me.

LITHERS. Hold up, Mr. Gabblewig.

GABBLEWIG. You might knock me down with a feather.

LITHERS. But you needn't knock *me* down with a barrister. Hold up, sir.

GABBLEWIG (*reading*). 'And her maid. Christopher Nightingale intends to try the cold-water cure.'

LITHERS. I beg your pardon, sir. What's his complaint?

GABBLEWIG. Nothing.

LITHERS (*shaking his head*). He'll never get over it, sir. Of all the invalids that come down here, the invalids that have nothing the matter with them are the hopeless cases.

GABBLEWIG (*reading*). 'Cold-water cure, having drunk (see Diary) four hundred and sixty-seven gallons, three pints and a half of the various celebrated waters of England and Germany, and proved them all to be humbugs. He has likewise proved (see Diary) all pills to be humbugs. Miss Rosina Nightingale, being rather low, will also try the cold-water cure, which will probably rouse her.'—Never!

Perhaps she, like me, may struggle with—

(And I have no doubt of it, Lithers, for she has the tenderest heart in the world)

Some feeling of regret

(awakened by the present individual).

But if she loved as I have loved,

(And I have no doubt she did—and does)

She never can forget.

(And she won't, I feel convinced, if it's only in obstinacy.) (*Gives back letter.*)

LITHERS. Well, sir, what'll you do? I'm entirely devoted to you, and ready to serve you in any way. Will you have a ladder from the builder's, and run away with the young lady in the middle of the night; or would the key of the street-door be equally agreeable?

GABBLEWIG. Neither. Can't be done. If it could be done I should have done it at Bath. Grateful duty won't admit of union without consent of uncle,—uncle won't give consent;—stick won't beat dog,—dog won't bite pig,—pig won't get over the stile;—and so the lovers will never be married! (*Sitting down as before.*) Give me the cold veal, and the day before yesterday's paper.

[*Exit* LITHERS, L., *and immediately returns with papers.*

SLAP (*without*). Halloa, here! My name is Formiville. Is Mr. Formiville's luggage arrived? Several boxes were sent on beforehand for Mr. Formiville; are those boxes here? (*Entering at door, preceded by* LITHERS, *who bows him in.*) Do you hear me, my man? Has Mr. Formiville's luggage—I am Mr. Formiville—arrived?

LITHERS. Quite safely, sir, yesterday. Three boxes, and a pair of foils.

SLAP. *And* a pair of foils. The same. Very good. Take this cap. (LITHERS *puts it down.*) Good. Put these gloves in the cap. (LITHERS *does so.*) Good. Give me the cap again, it's cold. (*He does so.*) Very good. Are you the landlord?

LITHERS. I am Thomas Lithers, the landlord, sir.

SLAP. Very good. You write in the title-pages of all your books, no doubt:—

> Thomas Lithers is my name,
> And landlord is my station;
> Malvern Wells my dwelling-place,
> And Chalk my occupation.

What have you got to eat, my man?

LITHERS. Well, sir, we could do you a nice steak; or we could toss you up a cutlet; or——

SLAP. What have you ready dressed, my man?

LITHERS. We have a very fine York ham, and a beautiful fowl, sir——

SLAP. Produce them! Let the banquet be served. Stay; have you——

LITHERS (*rubbing his hands*). Well, sir, we have, and I can strongly recommend it.

SLAP. To what may that remark refer, my friend?

LITHERS. I thought you mentioned Rhine-wine, sir.

SLAP. O truly. Yes, I think I did. Yes, I am sure I did. Is it very fine?

LITHERS. It is uncommon fine, sir. Liebfraumilch of the most delicious quality.

SLAP. You may produce a flask. The price is no consideration (*aside*)—as I shall never pay for it.

LITHERS. Directly, sir.

SLAP. So. He bites. He will be done. If he *will* be done he *must* be done. I can't help it. Thus men rush upon their fate. A stranger? Hum! Your servant, sir. My name is Formiville——

GABBLEWIG (*who has previously observed him*). Of several provincial theatres, I believe, and formerly engaged to assist an amateur company at Bath, under the management of——

SLAP (*with a theatrical pretence of being affected*). Mr. Gabblewig! Heavens! This recognition is so sudden, so unlooked for, —it unmans me. (*Aside.*) Owe him fifteen pounds, four shirts, and a waistcoat. Hope he's forgotten the loan of those trifles.—O sir, if I drop a tear upon that hand——

GABBLEWIG. Consider it done. Suppose the tear, as we used to say at rehearsal. How are you going on? You have left the profession?

SLAP (*aside*). Or the profession left me. I either turned *it* off, or *it* turned *me* off; all one. (*Aloud.*) Yes, Mr. Gabblewig, I am now living on a little property—that is, I have expectations—(*aside*) of doing an old gentleman.

GABBLEWIG. I have my apprehensions, Mr. Formiville, otherwise I believe, Mr. Slap——

SLAP. Slap, sir, was my father's name. Do not reproach me with the misfortunes of my ancestors.

GABBLEWIG. I was about to say, Slap, otherwise Formiville, that I have a very strong belief that you have been for some time established in the begging-letter-writing business. And when a gentleman of that description drops a tear on my hand, my hand has a tendency to drop itself on his nose.

SLAP. I don't understand you, sir.

GABBLEWIG. I see you don't. Now the danger is, that I, Gabblewig, may take the profession of the law into my own hands, and eject Slap, otherwise Formiville, from the nearest casement or window, being at a height from the ground not exceeding five-and-twenty feet.

SLAP (*angrily*). Sir, I perceive how it is. A vindictive old person, of the name of Nightingale, who denounced me to the Mendicity Society, and who has pursued me in various ways, has prejudiced your mind somehow, publicly or privately, against an injured and calumniated victim. But let that Nightingale beware; for, if the Nightingale is not a bird, though an old one, that I will catch yet once again with chaff, and clip the wings of, too, I'm—(*Aside.*) Confound my temper, where's it running? (*Affects to weep in silence.*)

GABBLEWIG (*aside*). Oho. That's what brings him here, is it? A trap for the Nightingales! I may show the old fellow that I have some purpose in me, after all!—Those amateur dresses among my baggage!—Lithers's assistance—done! Mr. Formiville.

SLAP (*with injured dignity*). Sir!

GABBLEWIG (*taking up hat and stick*). As I am not ambitious of the honour of your company, I shall leave you in possession of this apartment. I believe you are rather absent, are you not?

SLAP. Sir, I *am*, rather so.

GABBLEWIG. Exactly. Then you will do me the favour to observe that the spoons and forks of this establishment are the private property of the landlord.   [*Exit, L.*

SLAP. And that man wallows in eight hundred a year, and half that sum would make my wife and children (if I had any) happy!

Enter LITHERS (L.), *with tray, on which are fowl, ham, bread, and glasses.*

But arise, black vengeance! Nightingale shall suffer doubly. Nightingale found me out. When a man finds me out in imposing on him, I never forgive him,—and when he don't find me out, I never leave off imposing on him. Those are my principles. What ho! Wine here!

LITHERS (*arranging table and chair*). Wine coming, sir, directly! My young man has gone below for it. (*Bell rings without.*) More company! Mr. Nightingale, beyond a doubt! (*Showing him in at door.*) This way, sir, if you please! Your letter received, sir, and your rooms prepared.

SLAP (*looking off melodramatically before seating himself at table*). Is that the malignant whom these eyes have never yet bel-asted with a look? Caitiff, tereremble!

Sits, as NIGHTINGALE *enters with* ROSINA *and* SUSAN. NIGHTINGALE *muffled in a shawl, and carrying a great-coat.*

NIGHTINGALE (*to* LITHERS). That'll do, that'll do. Don't bother, sir. I am nervous, and can't bear to be bothered. What I want is peace. Instead of peace, I've got (*looking at* ROSINA) what

99

rhymes to it, and is not at all like it. (*Sits, covering his legs with his great-coat.*)

ROSINA. O uncle! Is it not enough that I am never to redeem those pledges which——

NIGHTINGALE. Don't talk to me about redeeming pledges, as if I was a pawnbroker! Oh! (*Starts.*)

ROSINA. Are you ill, sir!

NIGHTINGALE. Am I ever anything else, ma'am! Here! Refer to Diary (*gives book*). Rosina, save me the trouble of my glasses. See last Tuesday.

ROSINA. I see it, sir (*turning over leaves*).

NIGHTINGALE. What's the afternoon entry?

ROSINA (*reading*). 'New symptom. Crick in back. Sensation as if self a stiff boot-jack suddenly tried to be doubled up by strong person.'

NIGHTINGALE (*starts again*). O!

ROSINA. Symptom repeated, sir?

NIGHTINGALE. Symptom repeated. I must put it down. (SUSAN *brings chair, and produces screw-inkstand and pen from her pocket.* NIGHTINGALE *takes the book on his knee, and writes.*) 'Symptom repeated.'—Oh! (*Starts again.*) 'Symptom re-repeated.' (*Writes again.*) Mr. Lithers, I believe?

LITHERS. At your service, sir.

NIGHTINGALE. Mr. Lithers, I am a nervous man, and require peace. We had better come to an understanding. I am a water patient, but I'll pay for wine. You'll be so good as to call the pump sherry at lunch, port at dinner, and brandy-and-water at night. Now, be so kind as to direct the chambermaid to show this discontented young lady her room.

LITHERS. Certainly, sir. This way, if you please, Miss. (*He whispers her. She screams.*)

NIGHTINGALE (*alarmed*). What's the matter?

ROSINA. O uncle! I felt as if—don't be frightened, uncle,—as if something had touched me here (*with her hand upon her heart*) so unexpectedly, that I—don't be frightened, uncle—that I almost dropped, uncle.

NIGHTINGALE. Lord bless me! Boot-jack and strong person contagious! Susan, a mouthful of ink. (*Dips his pen in her inkstand, and writes.*) 'Symptom shortly afterwards repeated in niece.' Susan, *you* don't feel anything particular, do you?

SUSAN. Nothing whatever, sir.

NIGHTINGALE. You never do. You are the most aggravating young woman in the world.

SUSAN. Lor', sir, you wouldn't wish a party ill, I'm sure!

NIGHTINGALE. Ill! you *are* ill, if you only knew it. If you were as intimate with your own interior as I am with mine, your hair would stand on end.

SUSAN. Then I'm very glad of my ignorance, sir, for I wish it to keep in curl. Now, Miss Rosina! (*Exit* ROSINA, *making a sign of secrecy to* LITHERS, *who goes before*.) Oho! There's something in the wind that's not the boot-jack! [*Exit* SUSAN, L.

NIGHTINGALE (*seated*). There's a man, yonder, eating his dinner, as if he enjoyed it. I should say, from his figure, that he generally *did* enjoy his dinner. I wish I did. I wonder whether there is anything that would do me good. I have tried hot water, and hot mud, and hot vapour, and have imbibed all sorts of springs, from zero to boiling, and have gone completely through the pharmacopœia; yet I don't find myself a bit better. My Diary is my only comfort. (*Putting it into his great-coat pocket, unconsciously drops it*.) When I began to book my symptoms, and to refer back of an evening, then I began to find out my true condition. O! (*starts*) what's that? That's a new symptom. Lord bless me! Sensation as if small train of gunpowder sprinkled from left hip to ankle, and exploded by successful Guy Fawkes. I must book it at once, or I shall be taken with something else before it's entered. Susan, another mouthful of ink! Most extraordinary! [*Exit*, L.

(SLAP *cautiously approaches the Diary; as he does so,* GABBLEWIG *looks in and listens*.)

SLAP. What's this—hum! A Diary,—remarkable passion for pills, and quite a furor for doctors.—Very unconjugal allusions to Mrs. Nightingale.—Poor Maria, most valuable of sisters, to me an annuity,—to your husband a tormentor. Hum! shall I bleed him, metaphorically bleed him? Why not? He never regarded the claims of kindred; why should I? He returns. (*Puts down book*.)

Re-enter NIGHTINGALE, *looking about*.

NIGHTINGALE. Bless my heart, I've left my Diary somewhere. O! here is the precious volume—no doubt where I dropped it.

(*Picks up book.*) If the stranger had opened it, what information he might have acquired! He'd have found out, by analogy, things concerning himself that he little dreams of. He has no idea how ill he is, or how thin he ought to be.   [*Exit*, L.

SLAP. Now, then (*tucking up his wristbands*), for the fowl in earnest! Where is that wine! Hallo, where is that wine?

Enter (L.) GABBLEWIG, *disguised as Boots.*

GABBLEWIG. Here you are, sir! (*Starting.*) What do I behold! Mr. Formiville! the imminent tragedian?

SLAP. Who the devil are you? Keep off!

GABBLEWIG. What! Don't you remember me, sir?

SLAP. No, I don't indeed.

GABBLEWIG. Not wen I carried a banner, with a silver dragon on it; wen you played the Tartar Prince, at What's-his-name; and wen you used to bring the ouse down with that there pint about rewenge, you know?

SLAP. What! Do you mean when I struck the attitude, and said, 'Ar-recreant! The Per-rincess and r-r-revenge are both my own! She is my per-risoner—Tereremble!'

GABBLEWIG. Never! This to decide. (*They go through the motions of a broadsword combat.* SLAP, *having been run through the body, sits down and begins to eat voraciously.* GABBLEWIG, *who has kept the bottle all the while, sits opposite him at table.*) Ah! Lor' bless me, what a actor you was! (*Drinks.*) That's what I call true tragic fire—wen you strike it out of the swords. Give me showers of sparks, and then I know what you're up to! Lor' bless me, the way I've seen you perspire! I shall never see such a actor agin.

SLAP (*complacently*). I *think* you remember me.

GABBLEWIG. Think? Why, don't you remember, wen you left Taunton, without paying that there washerwoman; and wen she——

SLAP. You needn't proceed, it's quite clear you remember me.

GABBLEWIG (*drinks again*). Lor' bless my heart, yes, what a actor you was! What a Romeo you was, you know. (*Drinks again.*)

SLAP. I believe there was something in me, as Romeo.

GABBLEWIG. Ah! and something *of* you, too, you know. The Montagues was a fine family, when you was the lightest weight among 'em. And Lor' bless my soul, what a Prince Henry you was! I see you a drinking the sack now, I do! (*Drinks again.*)

SLAP. I beg your pardon, my friend, is that my wine?

GABBLEWIG (*affecting to meditate, and drinking again*). Lor' bless me, wot a actor! I seem to go into a trance like when I think of it. (*Is filling his glass again, when* SLAP *comes round and takes the bottle.*) I'll give you, Formiville and the Draymer! Hooray! (*Drinks, and then takes a leg of the fowl in his fingers.* SLAP *removes the dish.*)

SLAP (*aside*). At least he doesn't know that I was turned out of the company in disgrace. That's something. Are you the waiter here, my cool but discriminative acquaintance?

GABBLEWIG. Well, I'm a sort of a waiter and a sort of a half-boots: I was with a Travelling Circus, arter I left you. 'The riders—the riders! Be in time—be in time! Now, Mr. Merryman, all in to begin!' All that you know. But I shall never see acting no more. It went right out with you, bless you! (*All through this dialogue, whenever* SLAP, *in a moment of confidence, replaces the fowl or wine,* GABBLEWIG *helps himself.*)

SLAP (*aside*). I'll pump him—rule in life. Whenever no other work on hand, pump! (*To him.*) I forget your name.

GABBLEWIG. Bit—Charley Bit. That's my real name. When I first went on with the banners, I was Blitheringtonfordbury. But they said it came so expensive in the printing, that I left it off.

SLAP. Much business done in this house?

GABBLEWIG. Wery flat.

SLAP. Old gentleman in nankeen trousers been here long?

GABBLEWIG. Just come. Wot do you think I've heerd? S'posed to be a bachelor, but got a wife.

SLAP. No!

GABBLEWIG. Yes.

SLAP. Got a wife, eh? Ha, ha, ha! You're as sharp as a lancet. Ha, ha, ha! Yes, yes, no doubt. Got a wife. Yes, yes.

GABBLEWIG (*aside*). Eh! A flash! The intense enjoyment of my friend suggests to me that old Nightingale hasn't got a wife,—that he's free, but don't know it. Fraud! Mum! (*To him.*) I say, you're a—but Lor' bless my soul, wot a actor you wos!

SLAP. It's really touching, his relapsing into that! But I can't indulge him, poor fellow. My time is precious. You were going to say——

GABBLEWIG. I was going to say, you are up to a thing or two, and so—but, Lor' bless my heart alive, wot a Richard the Third you wos! Wen you used to come the sliding business, you know. (*Both starting up and doing it.*)

SLAP. This child of nature positively has judgment! It *was* one of my effects. Calm yourself, good fellow. 'And so'—you were observing——

GABBLEWIG (*close to him, in a sudden whisper*). And so I'll tell you. He hasn't really got a wife. She's dead. (SLAP *starts,—* GABBLEWIG *aside.*) I am right. He knows it! Mrs. Nightingale's as dead as a door-nail. (*A pause; they stand close together, looking at each other.*)

SLAP. Indeed? (*Gabblewig nods.*) Some piece of cunning, I suppose. (GABBLEWIG *winks.*) Buried somewhere, of course? (GABBLEWIG *lays his fingers on his nose.*) Where? (GABBLEWIG *looks a little disconcerted.*) All's safe. No proof. (*Aloud.*) Take away.

GABBLEWIG (*as he goes up to table*). Too sudden on my part. Formiville wins first knock-down blow. Never mind. Gabblewig up again, and at him once more. (*Clears the table and takes the tray away.*)

SLAP. How does *he* know? He's in the market. Shall I buy him? Not yet. Necessity not yet proved. With Nightingale here, and my dramatic trunks upstairs, I'll strike at least another blow on the hot iron for myself, before I think of taking a partner into the forge.   [*Exit*, L.

As GABBLEWIG *returns from clearing away, enter* SUSAN.

GABBLEWIG. Susan! Susan!

SUSAN. Susan, indeed! Well, diffidence ain't the prevailing complaint at Malvern.

GABBLEWIG. Don't you know me? Mr. Gabble——

SUSAN. —Wig! Why, la, sir, then *you're* the boot-jack! Now I understand, of course.

GABBLEWIG. More than I do. I the boot-jack! Susan, listen! Did you know that Mr. Nightingale had been married?

SUSAN. Why, I never heard it exactly.

GABBLEWIG. But you've seen it, perhaps? Had a peep into that eternal Diary—eh?

SUSAN. Well, sir, to say the pious truth, I did read one day something or another about a—a wife. You see he married a wife when he was very young.

GABBLEWIG. Yes.

SUSAN. And she was the plague of his life ever afterwards.

GABBLEWIG. O, Rosina, can such things be! Yes. Susan, I think you are a native of Malvern?

SUSAN. Yes, sir, leastways I was so, before I went to live in London.

GABBLEWIG. *You* persuaded Mr. Nightingale to come down here, in order that he might try the cold-water cure?

SUSAN. La, sir!

GABBLEWIG. And in order that you might see your relations?

SUSAN. La, sir, how did you know?

GABBLEWIG. Knowledge of human nature, Susan. Now rub up your memory and tell me—did you ever know a Mrs. Nightingale who lived down here? Think,—your eyes brighten,—you smile;—you did know Mrs. Nightingale who lived down here.

SUSAN. To be sure I did, sir; but that could never have been——

GABBLEWIG. Your master's wife,—I suspect she was. She died?

SUSAN. Yes, sir.

GABBLEWIG. And was buried?

SUSAN. You know everything.

GABBLEWIG. In——

SUSAN. Why, in Pershore churchyard; my uncle was sexton there.

GABBLEWIG. Uncle living?

SUSAN. Ninety years of age. With a trumpet.

GABBLEWIG. That he plays on?

SUSAN. Plays on? No. Hears with.

GABBLEWIG. Good. Susan, make it your business to get me a certificate of the old lady's death, and that within an hour.

SUSAN. Why, sir?

GABBLEWIG. Susan, I suspect the old lady walks, and I intend to lay her ghost. You ask how?

SUSAN. No, sir, I didn't.

GABBLEWIG. You thought it. That you shall know by and by. Here comes the old bird. Fly! (*Exit* SUSAN.) Whilst I reconnoitre the enemy.   [*Exit, through door.*

Enter NIGHTINGALE *and* ROSINA.

ROSINA. My dear uncle, pray do nothing rash : you are in capital health at present, and who knows what the doctors may make you.

NIGHTINGALE. Capital health? I've not known a day's health for these twenty years. (*Refers to Diary.*) 'January 6th, 1834. Pain in right thumb: query, gout. Send for Blair's pills. Take six. Can't sleep all night. Doze about seven.' (*Turns over leaf.*) 'March 12th, 1839: Violent cough: query, damp umbrella, left by church-rates in hall? Try lozenges. Bed at six—gruel—tallow nose—dream of general illumination. March 13th: Miserable': cold always makes me miserable. 'Receive a letter from Mrs. Nightin—' hem!

ROSINA. What did you say, sir?

NIGHTINGALE. Have the nightmare, my dear. (*Aside.*) Nearly betrayed myself! (*Aloud.*) You hear this, and you talk about capital health to a sufferer like me!

Enter SLAP, *at back, dressed as a smug physician.*
He appears to be looking about the room.

O! my spirits, my spirits! I wonder what water will do for them.

ROSINA. Why, reduce them, of course. Ah, my dear uncle, I often think I am the cause of your disquietude. I often think that I ought to marry.

NIGHTINGALE. Very kind of you, indeed, my dear.

Enter GABBLEWIG, *with a very large tumbler of water.*

O! all right, young man. I had better begin. So you think that you really ought, my love,—purely on my account—to marry a Magpie, don't you? (GABBLEWIG *starts and spills water over* NIGHTINGALE.) What are you about?

GABBLEWIG. I beg pardon, sir. (*Aside to* ROSINA.) Bless you!

ROSINA. Ah! Gab!—O uncle—don't be frightened—but——

NIGHTINGALE (*about to drink, spills water*). Return of boot-jack and strong person! I declare, I'm taking all this water externally, when I ought to——

SLAP (*seizing his hand*). Rash man, forbear! Drain that chalice, and your life's not worth a bodkin.

NIGHTINGALE. Dear me, sir! it's only water. I'm merely a pump patient. (GABBLEWIG *and* ROSINA *speak aside, hurriedly.*)

SLAP. Persevere, and twelve men of Malvern will sit upon you in

less than a week, and, without retiring, bring in a verdict of
'Found drowned.'

GABBLEWIG (*aside to* ROSINA). I have my cue, follow me directly.
I'll bring you another glass, sir, in a quarter of an hour.

> [*Exit at door.* ROSINA *steals after him.*

SLAP. A most debilitated pulse—(*taking away water*)—great
want of coagulum—lymphitic to an alarming degree. Stamina
(*strikes him gently*) weak—decidedly weak.

NIGHTINGALE. Right! Always was, sir. In '48,—I think it was '48
—(*Refers.*)—Yes, here it is. (*Reads.*) 'Dyspeptic. Feel as if
kitten at play within me. Try chalk and pea-flour.'

SLAP. And grow worse.

NIGHTINGALE. Astonishing! I did—yes. (*Reads.*)—'Fever—have
head shaved.'

SLAP. And grow worse.

NIGHTINGALE. Amazing! Sir, you read me like a book. As there
appears to be no dry remedy for my unfortunate case, I
thought I'd try a wet one; and here I am, at the cold
water.

SLAP. Water, unless in combination with alcohol, is poison to you.
You want blood. In man there are two kinds of blood. One in
a vessel called a vein, hence venous blood.—The other in the
vessel called artery; hence arterial blood—the one dark, the
other bright. Now, sir, the crassamentum of your blood is injured by too much water. How shall we thicken, sir? (*Produces bottle.*) By mustard and milk.

NIGHTINGALE. Mustard and milk!

SLAP. Mustard and milk, sir. Exhibited with a balsam known
only to myself. (*Aside.*) Rum! (*Aloud.*) Single bottles, one
guinea; case of twelve, ten pounds.

NIGHTINGALE. Mustard and milk! I don't think I ever tried—
Eh? Yes. (*Opens Diary.*) 1836; I recollect I once took—I took
—Oh, ah! 'Two quarts of mustard-seed, fasting.'

SLAP. Pish!

NIGHTINGALE. And you'd really advise me not to take water?

Enter at door GABBLEWIG *and* ROSINA, *both equipped in walking dresses, thick shoes, etc. They keep walking about during
the following.*

GABBLEWIG. Who says don't take water? Who says so?

107

NIGHTINGALE. Why, this gentleman, who is evidently a man of science.

GABBLEWIG. Pshaw! Eh, dear. Not take water! Look at us—look at us—Mr. and Mrs. Poulter. Six months ago, I never took water, did I, dear?

ROSINA. Never!

GABBLEWIG. Hated it. Always washed in gin-and-water, and shaved with spirits of wine. Didn't I, dear?

ROSINA. Always!

GABBLEWIG. Then what was I? What were *we*, I may say, my precious?

ROSINA. You may.

GABBLEWIG. A flabby, dabby couple, like a pair of wet leather gloves;—no energy—no muscle—no go-ahead. Now you see what we are; eh, dear? Ten miles before breakfast—home—gallon of water—ten miles more—gallon of water and leg of mutton,—ten miles more,—gallon of water—in fact, we're never quiet, are we, dear?

ROSINA. Never.

GABBLEWIG. Walk in our sleep—sometimes—can't walk enough, that's a fact, eh, dear?

ROSINA. Yes, dear!

SLAP. Confound this fellow, he'll spoil all.

NIGHTINGALE. Well, sir, if you really could pull up for a few minutes, I should be extremely obliged to you.

GABBLEWIG. Here we are, then,—don't keep us long. (*Looks at watch,* ROSINA *does the same.*)—Say a minute, chronometer time.

NIGHTINGALE. You must know I'm an invalid.

GABBLEWIG. Five seconds.

NIGHTINGALE. Come down here to try the cold-water cure.

GABBLEWIG. Ten seconds.

NIGHTINGALE. Dear me, sir, I wish you wouldn't keep counting the time in that way; it increases my nervousness.

GABBLEWIG. Can't help it, sir,—twenty seconds;—go on, sir.

NIGHTINGALE. Well, sir, this gentleman tells me that my cran-erany——

SLAP. Crass. Crassa-mentum must not be made too sloppy.

NIGHTINGALE. And thereby he advises, sir,——

108

GABBLEWIG. Forty seconds,—eh, dear? (*Show watches to each other.*)

ROSINA. Yes, dear!

NIGHTINGALE. I wish you wouldn't—and that he advises me to try mustard and milk, sir.

SLAP. In combination with a rare balsam known only to myself, one guinea a bottle,—case of twelve, ten pounds.

GABBLEWIG. Time's up. (*Walks again.*) My darling, mustard and milk? Eh, dear? Don't we know a case of mustard and milk,—Captain Blower, late sixteen stone, now ten and one half, all mustard and milk?

SLAP (*aside*). Can anybody have tried it?

GABBLEWIG (*to* NIGHTINGALE). Don't be done! If I see Blower, I'll send him to you;—can't stop longer, can we, dear?—ten miles and a gallon to do before dinner. Leg of mutton and a gallon at dinner. Five miles and a wet sheet after dinner. Come, dear! (*They walk out at door.*)

NIGHTINGALE. A very remarkable couple.—What do you think now, sir?

SLAP. Think, sir? I think, sir, that any man who professes to walk ten miles a day, is a humbug, sir; I couldn't do it.

NIGHTINGALE. But then the lady——

SLAP. I grieve to say that I think she's a humbugess. Those people, my dear sir, are sent about as cheerful examples of the effects of cold water. Regularly paid, sir, to waylay new comers.

NIGHTINGALE. La! do you think so? do you think there are people base enough to trade upon human infirmities?

SLAP. Think so?—I know it. There are men base enough to stand between you (*shows bottle*) and perfect health (*shakes bottle*) who would persuade you that perpetual juvenility was dear at one pound one a bottle, and that a green old age of a hundred and twenty was not worth ten pounds the case. That perambulating water-cart is such a man!

NIGHTINGALE. Wretch! What an escape I've had. My dear doctor. You are a doctor?

SLAP. D.D. and M.D., and corresponding member of the Mendicity Society.

NIGHTINGALE. Mendicity!

SLAP. Medical (what a slip).

NIGHTINGALE. Then I shall be happy to try a bottle to begin with. (*Gives money.*)

SLAP. Ah, one bottle. (*Gives bottle.*) I've confidence in your case, —you've none in mine. Ah! well!

NIGHTINGALE. A case be it then, and I'll pay the money at once. Permit me to try a little of the mixture. (*Drinks.*) It's not very agreeable. I think I'll make a note in my Diary of my first sensations.

Enter at door GABBLEWIG *and* ROSINA, *the former as a great invalid, the latter as an old nurse.*

GABBLEWIG (*aside, calling*). Rosina, quick, your arm. (*Aloud.*) I tell you, Mrs. Trusty, I can't walk any further.

ROSINA. Now do try, sir; we are not a quarter of a mile from home.

GABBLEWIG. A quarter of a mile!—why, that's a day's journey to a man in my condition.

ROSINA. O dear! what shall I do?

NIGHTINGALE. You seem very ill, sir?

GABBLEWIG. Very, sir. I'm a snuff, sir,—a mere snuff, flickering before I go out.

ROSINA. Oh, sir! pray don't die here; try and get home, and go out comfortably.

GABBLEWIG. Did you ever hear of such inhumanity? and yet this woman has lived on board wages, at my expense, for thirty years.

NIGHTINGALE. My dear sir, here's a very clever friend of mine who may be of service.

GABBLEWIG. I fear not,—I fear not. I've tried everything.

SLAP. Perhaps not *everything*. Pulse very debilitated; great want of coagulum; lymphitic to an alarming degree; stamina weak —decidedly weak.

GABBLEWIG. I don't want you to tell me that, sir.

SLAP. Crassamentum queer—very queer. No hope, but in mustard and milk.

GABBLEWIG (*starting up*). Mustard and milk!

ROSINA. Mustard and milk!

SLAP (*aside*). Is this Captain Blower?

GABBLEWIG (*to* NIGHTINGALE). Are you, too, a victim? Have you swallowed any of that man-slaughtering compound?

NIGHTINGALE (*alarmed*). Only a little,—a very little.

GABBLEWIG. How do you feel? Dimness of sight,—feeblesness of limbs?

NIGHTINGALE (*alarmed*). Not at present.

GABBLEWIG. But you will, sir,—you will. You'd never think I once rivalled that person, in rotundity.

NIGHTINGALE. Never.

ROSINA. But he'll never do it again; he'll never do it again.

GABBLEWIG. You'd never think that Madame Tussaud wanted to model my leg, and announce it as an *Extraordinary addition*.

NIGHTINGALE. I certainly should *not* have thought it.

GABBLEWIG. She might now put it in the Chamber of Horrors. Look at it!

ROSINA. It's nothing at all out of the flannel, sir.

GABBLEWIG. All mustard and milk, sir. I'm nothing but mustard and milk!

NIGHTINGALE (*seizes* SLAP). You scoundrel! and to this state you would have reduced me.

SLAP. O, this is some trick, sir, some cheat of the water-doctors.

NIGHTINGALE. Why, you won't tell me that he's intended as a cheerful example of the effects of cold water?

SLAP. I never said he was,—he's one of the failures; but as two of a trade can never agree, I'll go somewhere else and spend your guinea.   [*Exit.*

GABBLEWIG (*in his own voice*). What a brazen knave! Second knock-down blow to Gabblewig. Betting even. Anybody's battle. Gabblewig came up smiling and at him again.

NIGHTINGALE (*goes to* GABBLEWIG). My dear sir, what do I not owe you? (*Shakes his hand.*)

GABBLEWIG. O, don't do that, sir, I shall tumble to pieces like a fantoccini figure if you do. I am only hung together by threads.

NIGHTINGALE. But let me know the name of my preserver, that I may enter it in my Diary.

GABBLEWIG. Captain Blower, R.N. (NIGHTINGALE *writes.*) I'm happy to have rescued you from that quack. I declare the excitement has done me good. Rosi—Mrs. Trusty, I think I can walk now.

ROSINA. That's right, sir. Lean upon me.

GABBLEWIG. Oh! Oh!

NIGHTINGALE. What's the matter, Captain Blower?

GABBLEWIG. That's the milk, sir. Oh!

NIGHTINGALE. Dear me, Captain Blower!

GABBLEWIG. And that's the mustard, sir.

[*Exeunt at door* GABBLEWIG *and* ROSINA.

NIGHTINGALE. Really, this will be the most eventful day in my Diary, except one,—that day which consigned me to Mrs. Nightingale and twenty years of misery. I've not seen her for nineteen; though I have periodical reminders that she is still in the land of the living, in the shape of quarterly payments of twenty-five pounds, clear of income-tax. Well! I'm used to it; and so that I never see her face again, I'm content. I'll go find Rosina, and tell her what has happened. Quite an escape, I declare. [*Exit*, L.

Enter at door SUSAN, *in bonnet, etc.*

SUSAN. What a wicked world this is, to be sure! Everybody seems trying to do the best they can for themselves, and what makes it worse, the complaint seems to be catching; for I'm sure I can't help telling Mr. Gabblewig what a traitor that Tip is. I hope Mr. G. won't come in my way, and tempt me. Ah! here he is, and I'm sure I shall fall.

Enter GABBLEWIG.

GABBLEWIG. Well, Susan, have you got the certificate?

SUSAN. No, sir, but uncle has, and he'll be here directly. Oh, sir, if you knew what I've heard!

GABBLEWIG. What!

SUSAN. I'm sure you'd give half-a-sovereign to hear; I'm sure you would.

GABBLEWIG. I'm sure I should, and there's the money.

SUSAN. Well, sir, your man Tip's a traitor, sir, a conspirator, sir. I overheard him and another planning some deception. I couldn't quite make out what, but I know it's something to deceive Mr. Nightingale.

GABBLEWIG. Find out with all speed what this scheme is about, and let me know. What's that mountain in petticoats? Slap, or I'm not Gabblewig!

SUSAN. And with him Tip, or I'm not Susan!

GABBLEWIG. Another flash! I guess it all! Susan, your mistress shall instruct you what to do. Vanish, sweet spirit!

[*Exeunt* GABBLEWIG, R., *and* SUSAN, L.

Enter at door, R., SLAP *in female attire. Looks about cautiously.*

SLAP. I hope he's not gone out. I've a presentiment that my good luck is deserting me; but before we *do* part company, I'll make a bold dash, and secure something to carry on with. Now, Calomel,—I mean Mercury,—befriend me. (*Rings.*)

Enter LITHERS, L.

LITHERS. Did you ring, ma'am?
SLAP. Yes, young man; I wish to speak with a Mr. Nightingale, an elderly gent, who arrived this morning.
LITHERS. What name, ma'am?
SLAP. Name no consequence; say I come from M'ria.
LITHERS. M'ria?
SLAP. M'ria, a mutual friend of mine and Mr. Nightingale, and one he ought not to be ashamed of.
LITHERS. Yes, ma'am. (*Aside.*) Mr. Gabblewig's right.   [*Exit.*
SLAP. M'ria has been dead these twelve years, during which time my victim has paid her allowance with commendable regularity to me, her only surviving brother. Ah, I thought that name was irresistible, and here he is.

Enter NIGHTINGALE, L., *closing door at back.*

His trepidation is cheering. He'll bleed freely; what a lamb it is! (*Curtseys as* NIGHTINGALE *comes down.*) Your servant, sir.
NIGHTINGALE. Now don't lose a moment; you say you come from Maria: what Maria?
SLAP. Your Maria.
NIGHTINGALE. I am sorry to acknowledge the responsibility.
SLAP. Ah, sir; that poor creature's much changed, sir.
NIGHTINGALE. For the worse, of course?
SLAP. I'm afraid so. No gin now, sir.
NIGHTINGALE. Then it's brandy.
SLAP. Lives on it, sir, and breaks more windows than ever. She's heard that you've come down here.
NIGHTINGALE. So I suppose, by this visit.
SLAP. She lives about a mile from Malvern.

113

NIGHTINGALE (*starts*). What! I thought she was down in York-
shire.

SLAP. Was and is is two different things. She wanted for to come
and see you.

NIGHTINGALE. If she does, I'll stop her allowance.

SLAP. And have her call every day? M'ria's my friend,—but I
know that wouldn't be pleasant. She'd a proposal to make, so,
M'ria says I,—I'll see your lawful husband,—as you is, sir, and
propose for you.

NIGHTINGALE. I'll listen to nothing.

SLAP. Not if it puts the sad sea-waves between you and M'ria for
ever?

NIGHTINGALE (*interested*). Eh!

SLAP. You know she'd a brother, an excellent young man, who
went to America ten years ago.

NIGHTINGALE (*takes out Diary*). I know. (*Reads aside.*) '16th of
May 1841, sent fifty pounds to Mrs. N.'s vagabond brother,
going to America—qy. to the devil?'

SLAP. He has written to M'ria to say that if you'll give her two
hundred pounds, and she'll come out, he'll take care of her
for ever.

NIGHTINGALE. Done!—it's a bargain.

SLAP. *He bites!*—and her son for a hundred more.

NIGHTINGALE. What son?

SLAP. Ah, sir! you don't know your blessings. Shortly after you
and M'ria separated, a son was born; but M'ria, to revenge
herself—which was wrong; oh, it was wrong in her, that was,
—never let you know it; but sent him to the Workus, as a
fondling she had received in a basket.

NIGHTINGALE. I don't believe a word of it.

SLAP. She said you wouldn't. But seeing is believing, and so I've
brought the innocent along with me. I've got the Pretty here.

NIGHTINGALE. Here! in your pocket?

SLAP. No—at the door. (*They rise.*)

NIGHTINGALE. At the door!

SLAP. Come in, Christopher! Named after you, sir! for in spite
of M'ria's feelings, you divided her heart with Old Tom.

Enter at door TIP *as a Charity Boy.*

NIGHTINGALE. O nonsense!

114

SLAP. Christopher, behold your Par. (*Boxes him.*) What do you stand there for like a eight-day clock or a idol, as if Pars were found every day?

TIP (*aside*). Don't; you make me nervous. (*Aloud.*) And is that my Par!

SLAP. Yes, child. Me, who took you from the month, can vouch for it.

TIP. O Par!

NIGHTINGALE. Keep off, you young yellow-hammer; or I'll knock you down. Hark'ee, ma'am. If you can assure me of the departure of your friend and this cub, I will give you the money! For twenty years I have been haunted by——

Enter GABBLEWIG *at door, disguised as Old Woman.*

GABBLEWIG. Which the blessed innocent has been invaygled of, and man-trapped,—leastways boy-trapped;—and never no more will I leave this 'ouse until I find a parent's 'ope—a mother's pride—and nobody's (as I'm aweer on) joy.

NIGHTINGALE *and Susan place Chair.*

SLAP (*aside*). What on earth is this! Who is a mother's pride and nobody's joy? (*To* TIP.) You don't mean to say you are?

TIP (*solemnly*). I'm a horphan. (*Goes up to* GABBLEWIG.) What are you talking about, you old Bedlam?

GABBLEWIG. Oh! (*screaming and throwing her arms about his neck*)—my 'ope—my pride—my son!

TIP (*struggling*). Your son!

GABBLEWIG (*aside to him*). If you don't own me for your mother, you villain, on the spot, I'll break every bone in your skin, and have your skin prepared afterwards by the Bermondsey tanners.

TIP (*aside*). My master!—My mother! (*They embrace.*)

SLAP. Are you mad? Am I mad? Are we all mad? (*To* TIP.) Didn't you tell me that whatever I said——

TIP. *You* said? What is your voice to the voice of Natur? (*Embraces his master again.*)

SLAP. Natur! Natur! ah-h-h! (*Screams. Chair brought.*) O you unnat'ral monster! Who see your first tooth drawn on a deceitful world? Who watched you running alone in a go-cart, and

115

tipping over on your precious head upon the paving-stones in the confidence of childhood? Who give you medicine that reduced you when you was sick, and made you so when you wasn't?

GABBLEWIG (*rising*). Who? Me!

SLAP. You, ma'am?

GABBLEWIG. Me, ma'am, as is well beknown to all the country round, which the name of this sweetest of babbies as was giv to his own joyful self when blest in best Whitechapel mixed upon a pincusheon, and mother saved likewise was Absolom. Arter his own parential father, as never (otherwise than through being bad in liquor) lost a day's work in the wheelwright business, which it was but limited, Mr. Nightingale, being wheels of donkey shays and goats, and one was even drawed by geese for a wager, and went right into the centre aisle of the parish church on a Sunday morning on account of the obstinacy of the animals, as can be certified by Mr. Wigs the beadle afore he died of drawing on his Wellington boots, to which he was not accustomed, arter a hearty meal of beef and walnuts, to which he was too parshal, and in the marble fountain of that church this preciousest of infants was made Absolom, which never can be unmade no more, I am proud to say, to please or give offence to no one nowheres and no-hows.

SLAP. Would you forswear your blessed mother, M'ria Nightingale, lawful wedded wife of this excellent old gent? Why don't the voice o' Natur claim its par?

NIGHTINGALE. O, don't make *me* a consideration on any account!

GABBLEWIG. M'ria Nightingale, which affliction sore long time she bore——

NIGHTINGALE. And so did I.

GABBLEWIG. Physicians was in vain,—which she never had none partickler as I knows, of exceptin one which she tore his hair by handfuls out in consequence of differences of opinion relative to her complaint, but it was wrote upon her tombstone ten year and more ago, and dead she is as the hosts of the Egyptian Fairies.

NIGHTINGALE. Dead! Prove it, and I'll give you fifty pounds.

SLAP. Prove it! I defies her. (*Aside.*) I'm done.

GABBLEWIG. Prove it!—which I can and will, directly minit, by

116

my brother the sexton, as I will here produce in the twinkling of a star or human eye. (*Aside.*) From this period of the contest Gabblewig had it all his own way, and went in and won. No money was laid out, at any price, on Formiville. Fifty to one on Gabblewig freely offered, and no takers. [*Exit at door.*

SLAP (*aside*). I don't like this,—so exit Slap!

NIGHTINGALE (*seizing him*). No, ma'am, you don't leave this place till the mystery is cleared up.

SLAP. Unhand me, monster! I claims my habeas corpus. (*Breaks from him.* NIGHTINGALE *goes to the door and prepares to defend the pass with a chair.*) (*To* TIP.) As for you, traitor, though I'm not pugnacious, I'll give you a lesson in the art of self-defence you shall remember as long as you live.

TIP. You! the bottle imp as has been my ruin! Reduce yourself to my weight, and I'll fight you for a pound. (*Squares.*)

GABBLEWIG (*without*). I'll soon satisfy the gentleman.

SLAP. Then I'm done! very much done! I see nothing before me but premature incarceration, and an old age of gruel.

Enter GABBLEWIG *at door as Sexton.*

NIGHTINGALE. He's very old! My invaluable centenarian, will you allow me to inquire——

SEXTON. I don't hear you.

NIGHTINGALE. He's very deaf. (*Aloud.*) Will you allow me to inquire——

SEXTON. It's no use whispering to me, sir, I'm hard o' hearing.

NIGHTINGALE. He's very provoking. (*Louder.*) Whether you ever buried——

SEXTON. Brewed? Yes, yes, I brewed—that is, me and my wife, as has been dead and gone now this forty year, next hop-picking—(my wife was a Kentish woman)—we brewed, especially one year, the strongest beer ever you drunk. It was called in our country Sampson with his hair on—alluding to its great strength, you understand,—and my wife, she said——

NIGHTINGALE (*very loud*). Buried—not brewed!

SEXTON. Buried? O, ah! Yes, yes. Buried a many. They was strong, too,—once.

NIGHTINGALE. Did you ever bury a Mrs. Nightingale?

SEXTON. Ever bury a Nightingale? No, no, only Christians.

NIGHTINGALE (*in his ear*). Missis—Mis-sis Nightingale?

117

SEXTON. O yes, yes. Buried *her*—rather a fine woman,—married (as the folks told me) an uncommon ugly man. Yes, yes. Used to live here. Here (*taking out pocket-book*) is the certificate of her burial. (*Gives it.*) I got it for my sister. O yes! Buried *her*. I thought you meant a Nightingale. Ha, ha, ha!

NIGHTINGALE. My dear friend, there's a guinea, and it's cheap for the money. (*Gives it.*)

SEXTON. I thank'ee, sir. I thank'ee. (*Aside.*) Formiville heavily grassed, and a thousand to one on Gabblewig! [*Exit at door.*

NIGHTINGALE (*after reading certificate*). You—you—inexpressible swindler. If you were not a woman, I'd have you ducked in the horse-pond.

TIP (*on his knees*). O, sir, do it. He deserves it.

NIGHTINGALE. He?

TIP. Yes, sir, she's a he. He deluded me with a glass of rum-and-water; and the promise of a five-pound note.

NIGHTINGALE. You scoundrel!

SLAP. Sir, you are welcome to your own opinion. I am not the first man who has failed in a great endeavour. Napoleon had his Waterloo,—Slap has his Malvern. Henceforth, I am nobody. The eagle retires to his rock.

Enter GABBLEWIG *in his own dress.*

GABBLEWIG. You had better stop here. Be content with plain Slap,—discard counterfeit Formiville,—and we'll do something for you.

SLAP. Mr. Gabblewig! [*Exit at door.*

GABLEWIG. Charley Bit, Mr. Poulter, Captain Blower, respectable female, and deaf sexton, all equally at anybody's service.

NIGHTINGALE. What do I hear?

GABBLEWIG. Me.

NIGHTINGALE. And what do I see?

ROSINA (*entering at door*). Me! Dear uncle, you would have been imposed upon and plundered, and made even worse than you ever made yourself, but for——

GABBLEWIG. Me. My dear Mr. Nightingale, you did think I could do nothing but talk. If you now think I can act—a little—let me come out in a new character. (*Embracing* ROSINA.) Will you?

NIGHTINGALE. Will I? Take her, Mr. Gabblewig. Stop, though.

Ought I to give away what has made me so unhappy. Memorandum—Mrs. Nightingale—see Diary. (*Takes out book.*)

GABBLEWIG. Stop, sir! Don't look! Burn that book, and be happy!—-(*Brings on* SLAP *at door.*)—Ask your doctor. What do *you* say, Mustard and Milk?

SLAP. I say, sir, try me; and when you find I am not worth a trial, don't try me any more. As to that gentleman's destroying his Diary, sir, my opinion is that he might perhaps refer to it once again.

GABBLEWIG (*to audience*). Shall he refer to it once more? (*To* NIGHTINGALE.) Well, I think you may.

CURTAIN